ESSAYS IN LINGUISTICS:
Studies in Phonology, Syntax and Sociolinguistics

Essays in Linguistics:
Studies in Phonology, Syntax and Sociolinguistics

Shyamal Das

AKANSHA PUBLISHING HOUSE
NEW DELHI-110002 (INDIA)

AKANSHA PUBLISHING HOUSE
4649-B/21, Ansari Road
Darya Ganj, New Delhi - 110 002
Ph.: 23263193 / 9811582579 / 09435116718
Telefax: 011-23263193
Email: ektabooks@yahoo.com
www.akanshapublishinghouse.com

Essays in Linguistics: Studies in Phonology, Syntax and Sociolinguistics

First Published 2009
ISBN 978-81-8370-184-6

PRINTED IN INDIA

Published by Akansha Publishing House, New Delhi and Printed at Aryan Enterprises, Delhi.

Contents

Foreword

It is a common experience in the third world countries that linguistic research is primarily focused on the standard varieties. This is because given the paucity of interest and incentives both at the individual and societal level, whatever resources are available, get directed towards the standard variety. As a result the huge number of dialects or 'real languages' fail to come to the limelight of linguistic studies. But ever since the emergence of the generative linguistics, researchers world wide unanimously have accorded the status of 'language' to any verbal system through which successful communication is carried out by its native speakers. In virtue of this, the grammatical properties of any verbal system could be made the subject of indepth research and the results of such studies definitely hold promises for providing rich insights about the nature of Universal Grammar or UG.

Dialectal difference within the same language yields to parametric variation at par with the attributes of language typology. Additionally, interdialectal variations which occupies a central place in dialectology, also holds a significant key to theorizing on the properties of language change: weakening at both segmental and prosodic levels is one such putative feature of language change. On the top of it all, a principled account of language variation helps the users of various dialects to understand each other better even as it holds promises to contribute substantially to promoting linguistic harmony and amity especially in a multilingual context such as that prevailing in a country like India.

In the present collection of papers, the focus has been primarily on explaining the phonological variations between the eastern and the western dialects of Bangla. For the latter, the Standard Colloquial Bangla or SCB has been taken as the model while for the former the dialects of Bangla spoken in different parts of Tripura provide the specimens for variant systems. Beside these studies in dialectal phonology, aspects of Bangla syntax have also drawn our attention. Certain issues relating to the language problems of the tribal folks of the state have been given some serious thoughts from the perspectives of socio- and ethno-linguistics.

One of my particular areas of interest being (synchronic) language change, I have tried to pinpoint the major changes at work across dialects of a language, in this case Bangla. It has been found that it is primarily the domain of phonology where the processes of variations are predominantly initiated. The most common process signifying change is weakening or lenition of various sorts. At the prosodic level weakening results in stress dispersion giving rise to ternary or even unbounded feet. At the segmental level, weakening targets consonants which undergo phase-wise lenition: stop → fricatives → glotalization → vocalizaiton → null e.g. in Tripura Bangla subvarieties k → χ → h → 0 as in dokan (Standard Colloquial Bangla) → doχan (Sylheti Bangla) → dohan (Cumilla/Agartala/Tripura Bangla) → doan (Noakhali Bangla) 'shop' etc. Perhaps in course of time it would be possible to make a stronger claim in favour of weakening being a canonical feature of distinction between the standard and the non-standard dialects of a language. The present study seeks to provide further empirical support in favour of this stand.

In Bangla segmental phonology, two dialects the standard one i.e. Standard Colloquial Bangla and a non-standard one namely Noakhali Bangla (or NKB) examined in the paper "Who is Afraid of Noakhali Bangla?", show significant differences. In respect of consonants it is found that:

(1) the entire set of SCB voiced aspirated stops /b^h, d^h, $ɖ^h$, g^h/ is lost in NKB;

(2) /p^h/ cannot be treated as part of the underlying inventory of the language, because although /p^h/ exists in principle it is

never phonetically realized: it is neutralized to [h] word initially and to [p] elsewhere;

(3) /p pʰ/ and optionally /ʃ/ weaken to [h];

(4) the SCB [h] is lost in NKB and the one found in NKB is only a derived segment with no existence in the underlying inventory;

(5) the SCB affricates /c cʰ/ and /j jʰ/ get fricativized and fronted to /s/ and /z/ respectively;

(6) the SCB retroflex flap /ɽ/ is phonetically simplified to [r] in NKB;

(7) none of the dialects can be said to have clear cut evidence of semivowels.

The neat result of all these is that the NKB consonantal inventory stands drastically reduced to nineteen: with eight non-aspirated stops /p b t d ʈ ɖ k g/, three voiceless aspirated stops /tʰ ʈʰ kʰ/, three fricatives /s z ʃ/, three nasals /m n ŋ/, and one flap /r/ and one lateral /l/. SCB by contrast has twenty eight consonants consisting of sixteen plosives equally divided between aspirated and unaspirated ones /p b t d ʈ ɖ k g pʰ bʰ tʰ dʰ ʈʰ ɖʰ kʰ gʰ/, four affricates /c j cʰ jʰ/, two fricatives /ʃ h/, three nasals /m n ŋ/, two flaps /r ɽ/ and one lateral /l/.

In case of vowels it has been noted that while SCB is a seven vowel system with /i e æ a ɔ o u/, NKB is a six vowel one containing /i æ a ɔ o u/. Additionally, both the systems utilize nasality for phonemic contrast. In respect of complex vowels both use diphthongs both oral and nasal. Once again the two dialects differ notably: while SCB has seventeen oral diphthongs with phonemic status namely /ui, ei, ai, oi, au, eu, ia, ua, oa, ɔa, ea, ɛo, eo, ao, ɔe, ɔo, iu/, NKB has sixteen /ui, ei, ai, oi, au, eu, ia, ua, oa, ɔa, ea, iɔ, ɛə, aɔ, oɔ, uɔ/. As for nasal diphthongs SCB has sixteen /ũĩ, ẽĩ, ãĩ, õĩ, ãũ, ẽũ, ĩã, õã, ẽã, ɛ̃õ, ẽõ, ãõ, ɔ̃ẽ, õũ/, [ɔ̃õ], [ĩũ] of which nasality in the last two are contextually conditioned i.e. they acquire nasality from the preceding nasal consonant. In NKB, on the other hand, there are thirteen nasal diphthongs /ũĩ, ẽĩ, ãĩ, õĩ, ãũ, ẽũ, ĩã, õã, ẽã, ũã, ɔ̃ã, ĩɔ̃ õɔ̃/ all enjoying phonemic status.

An interesting observation impinging on the issue of language change is the emergence of a High tone to compensate for the loss of the feature aspiration or [spr.gl] from the feature matrix for consonants. Beside this, there are found ample examples of vowel length being used contrastively in NKB, and such lengthening becomes operational both in consonance with and without tone, resulting in a sizable number of free variants. Given this rather confusing picture it requires further investigation to ascertain whether vowel lengthening is only a phonetic i.e. a surface phenomenon or it is gradually percolating deep down into the core phonology of featural distinctions in NKB. One of the offshoots of this drastically reduced number of consonants and, conversely, a large number of vowels (six oral monophthongs, six nasal monophthongs, sixteen oral diphthongs, and thirteen nasal diphthongs) along with distinctive vowel length and a High tone making up for the loss of aspiration, is that NKB appears to be a system distinctly vowel-dominated. The phenomenon of consonant weakening and deletion (discussed in Das 1996) so common in this dialect, produces innumerable cases of vowel coalescence resulting in sequences of three and four vowels. The cumulative effect of all these is that the dialect sounds a rather exotic one to the non-NKB speakers, endangering intelligibility and communication. In addition, the role of prosody (i.e. syllable template, foot pattern, nature of stress assignment — iterative or non-iterative, bounded or un-bounded etc.) when examined in detail, may throw further light on this overall reductionist tendency of the NKB speakers. Such a study acquires special significance in the light of the upcoming theories like perceptual salience (cf. Cote 1997, 2000a, 2000b, 2001, 2004, Hume 1999, Fleming 1995, Steriade 1999 etc.) where consonants have an edge over vowels in respect of conveying lexical information.

In the second article "Why does Tripura Bangla Sound so Different from Standard Bangla?" I focus on a contrastive scenario prevailing in the vowel inventories of the verbal stems in SCB and TB. The former has done away with the high vowel i, u while the latter strongly retains them. By contrast, while TB has nearly wiped out e, o, SCB tends to accord them almost the status of the *unmarked.* What makes the picture in TB an intriguing one is the presence of the isolated remnants of the otherwise diminishing vowels e, o. Investigation has traced these remnants in positions, which are traditionally recognized as prosodic heads. The latter are notorious for licensing certain phonological processes even as they block others (cf. Beckman 1997, 1998, Kager 1999 etc.). The latter is therefore responsible for blocking an otherwise well-attested process of vowel neutralization in TB.

"Why do the People of Tripura Speak so Fast?" is focused on explaining the phenomenon of ternary rhythm in the area of prosodic phonology. In comparison to binary rhythm, ternary rhythm is a marked pattern of metrification noticed in only a handful of world languages. Many proposals have been made for giving a principled account of this phenomenon of metrical dispersion such as TERNARY FEET (Halle and Vergnaud 1987, Levin 1988, Dresher & Lahiri 1991, Hewitt 1992, Rice 1992); binary feet with a special parsing mode called Weak Local Parsing (Hayes 1995), Relativized Extrametricality (Hammond 1990); in the Optimality Theory or OT framework, a foot-repulsion constraint *FTFT (Kager 1994). In recent times the analytical perspective on ternary rhythm has witnessed a radical change. Capitalizing on the idea that ternarity is not a primitive of metrical phonology, efforts have been made to derive ternary rhythm with binary feet through interaction of foot alignment (ALL-FT-X) with an anti-lapse constraint (Ishii 1996). However, the entire theoretical artifice is crucially dependent on an appropriate statement of the anti-lapse constraint. One such approach to defining the anti-lapse constraint is the grid-based lapse constraint *LAPSE (Elenbaas 1999, Elenbaas and Kager 1999) which has proved its mettle in offering a principled and unified account of rhythmic ternarity in many a language. A welcome feature of this constraint is that it is not specific to any particular rhythm in the sense that it broadly enforces bounded rhythm, either binary or ternary. But despite its spectacular success both empirically and typologically, *LAPSE is unable to account for the presence of a word-final triple upbeat in the trochaic system of

Tripura Bangla, spoken in the Indian state of Tripura. Explaining this metrical pattern requires a reformulation of the anti-lapse constraint such that only the edges of two prosodic domains - foot and word - function as valid licensors of weak beats. In this respect it differs from the earlier version conveniently renamed *LAPSE (E&K) which allows the strong beat and the word-edge to license weak beats in a grid. The main thrust of the present study is the newly defined lapse constraint *LAPSE(DE) where DE stands for *domain edges*. The advantage of *LAPSE(DE) is that it not only succeeds in accommodating the *deviant* facts of TB but also accounts for all the cross-linguistic data that provided the empirical justification to *LAPSE (Elenbaas and Kager). Hence is the superiority of the former over the latter.

Next article "The 'Lazy' Speakers of Standard Bangla" continues the search into the prosodic phenomenon of TB as opposed to SCB. Research in typology of word stress has shown that 'stress patterns are a domain of potentially conflicting forces such as rhythm, quantity sensitivity and edge-marking.' Systems may or may not comply with all these three pressures, but the situation becomes intriguing when two cognate systems instantiate two different possibilities: one obeying and the other ignoring all or some of them. The two systems under reference are the two dialects of Bangla namely, SCB and TB. In the former there is a strong rhythmicity requirement accompanied by quantity sensitivity. It also observes edge-marking although partially. By contrast, its cognate TB does not appear to yield to any of such pressures. Any theory of metrical phonology staking its claim on predictability as well as explanatory adequacy must be able to meet such a challenge with a unified theory of grammar as the two systems belong to the same language *viz* Bangla. In the present paper such a theory is proposed in terms of variable ranking of an almost identical set of constraints to account for the disparity prevailing in the two dialects of Bangla under study. Obviously the theoretical framework is the OT as propounded by McCarthy and Prince (1993) and Prince and Smolensky (1993), and other subsequent illustrations.

"Bangla: A Language without Subject and Object — A Study in Pro-drop Phenomenon" explores a rather unique phenomenon of Bangla syntax i.e. non-mandatory requirement for the surface realization of the Subject and Object Noun Phrases or (NPs). Chomsky (1982) classifies NPs in terms of two features [± Anaphor] and [± Pronominal]. On the basis of these two features, each specified as either [+] or [-], there are four possible combinations containing both overt and covert NPs as shown below.

Type	Overt	Non-overt
[+A, -P]	Anaphor	NP-trace
[-A, +P]	Pronoun	pro
[-A, -P]	R-expression	Wh-trace
[+A, +P]	——	PRO

Of these non-overt NPs, NP-trace and Wh-traces are derived through movements, PRO is base-generated. An NP-trace, like an anaphor is bound within its Governing Category (henceforth GC) by an antecedent from an Argument position as required by principle A of Binding Theory. A Wh-trace is like an R-expression and in compliance with the Binding Principles C, it is free in the GC in the sense that it is bound by its antecedent in a non-Argument position (hence forth Ā-position). PRO is a base generated empty category which vacuously satisfies both Principle A and B by occurring in a position which is ungoverned and PRO fails to have any GC at all. Finally, coming to the non-overt corollary to the combination [-A, +P] the generative linguists have identified it as *pro*. It is subject to Principle B of Binding Theory (cf. Chomsky, 1982:78). *pro* is governed and its content is recoverable from syntactic clues provided in the sentence.

Italian provides good examples of such empty category. Let us consider the following sentences from Italian.

1. Gianni ha parlato
   'Gianni has spoken.'

2. e Ha parlato
   '*Has spoken.'

3. Gianni ha ditto [che [e ha parlato]]
                          CP   IP
   '*Gianni has said that   has spoken'

In (1) *parlato* assigns its θ-role to Gianni. By analogy we assume that the same is true about (2) and (3) also. On the basis of the Extended PP we postulate that there is a subject position namely [Spec. IP], in all the examples (1-3) above. The projected subject position of *ha parlato* in (1) is an NP position which is not phonetically realized and in which the external θ-role of the verb is realized. We assume therefore, that the [Spec. IP] position is occupied by a zero element. The zero element however cannot be a trace as it does not have an antecedent. Nor can it be a PRO because PRO must be ungoverned while the finite inflexion in (2) and (3) definitely govern *e*. The *e* in (2) however has a definite reference. Like a pronoun it may refer to an entity in the non-linguistic context or it may be co-indexed with an element in the linguistic context. In (3) one possible interpretation is that the non-overt subject of *ha parlato* is identical to that of the overt subject of *ha detto*. In brief, the non-overt subject in (2) and (3) is the missing non-overt NP i.e. the non-overt pronoun. It has the feature [-A, +P] and is represented by *pro*.

It is instructing to note that every language does not allow *pro*. A language like Italian (also Spanish) uses *pro* as the properties of this phonetically unrealized NP can be recovered from the rich agreement features. But as Huang (1984) has shown a language like Chinese or Japanese which entirely lacks in inflection also allows *pro*-drop. Borer (1980, 1983 and 1986) on the other hand has showed that Modern Hebrew makes only a limited application of the *pro*-drop phenomenon. Instead of going, therefore, into the details of this controversy as to what criteria exactly enable a language to drop *pro* the aim in the present paper would be to make a survey of the SCB (or Bangla in brief) as it is spoken in and around Kolkata to examine if it observes the *pro*-drop phenomenon. For this purpose we take both Italian and

English as standards to provide both comparative and contrastive illustrations.

In the section containing essays on sociolinguistics, the first one "Standardization or the Politics of Marginalization: A Study in the Light of Freedom of Speech and Expression" addresses the issue of standardization and its corollary linguistic marginalization. Identity and identification are, ironically, antithetical. Quest for identity is conceptually centrifugal and often gives rise to new centres. Rise of every new centre, because it is ontologically defined by a circle, presumes the loss of many micro centres within or outside the circle. Every such loss of identity contributes to the process of identification. This tension between identity and identification, between the individual identity and collective identity, between micro and macro is perhaps a universal phenomenon since every human being is an individual living, not in isolation, but in society. The present paper seeks to study this aspect of tension between *the one* and *the many* in the arena of language—the most crucial mark of one's identity. There is no language as such in this world because every language is only a dialect 'fortunate enough' to acquire the status of the standard one. But study reveals that lots of maneuverings are involved in the process of standardization. And standardization of *the one*, obviously implies the marginalization of *the many*. This article explores some of these factors and the consequences of standardization with reference to the linguistic scenario in Tripura in particular.

Finally, the article "Is De-centering for De-centering Well-centered?" can be treated as a rejoinder to the proposition made in the preceding article. If it is easy to sentimentalize the issue of identity built around one's language, it is easier to fall a prey to emotional blackmailing and play the stooge in the hands of subversive forces. In this postmodern era, the subaltern's quest for identity often tends to go to any extreme in order to become 'absolutely' free from the hegemony of the centre. But before long in the absence of any well thought out and time-tested guiding principles from within, and because no vacuum remains for long in nature's disposition, the wild zeal of revolution becomes susceptible to the lure offered by alternative centres. The latter thus find an obedient 'wild force' at its control to carry out its vested agenda. Choosing between the centres thus becomes an extremely important issue in respect of identity quest for the marginalized. This last article in this collection attempts to have a closer look at the tribal language scenario of Tripura in relation to this theoretical issue of alternative identity.

List of Abbreviations and Constraints

A	Anaphor
AGR	Agreement features
ALIGN (Leftmost)	The head foot is leftmost in the Prosodic Word
ALIGN-L	ALIGN-LEFT or Align (PrWd-L,Ft-L)
ALL-FT-L	Every foot stands at the left edge of the Prosodic Word.
ALL-FT-L/R	The edge X of every foot coincides with the edge X of some PrWd.
*CLASH	No stressed syllables are adjacent'
*CLASH-FT or *FT-FT	Feet must not be adjacent.
CB	Cumilla Dialect of Bangla
CP	Complementizer Phrase
DEP-σ-IO	Output syllables have input correspondents.
DEP-μ-IO	Output moras have input correspondents.
DISYL-FT	Disyllabic Foot
e	Empty category
EPP	Extended Projection Principle
FT-BIN	Feet are binary at some level of analysis (μ, σ).
GC	Governing Category

GrWd	:	Grammatical Word
H	:	Heavy syllable
INFL	:	INFLEXION
IP	:	Inflexion Phrase
L	:	Light syllable
*LAPSE	:	Every weak beat must be adjacent to a strong beat or the word-edge.
*LAPSE (DE)	:	Every weak beat must be adjacent either to a *directional foot-edge* or word-edge.
LGB	:	Lectures on Government and Binding
*LINK-μ-to-[+cons]	:	Consonants are not moraic.
MAX-μ-IO	:	Input moras have output correspondents.
NKB	:	Noakhali Dialect of Bangla
MSA	:	Modern Standard Arabic
NON-FIN	:	Non-Finality
OT	:	Optimality Theory
P	:	Pronoun
PAR-SYL	:	Syllables are parsed by feet.
pro	:	Pronoun
PrWd	:	Prosodic Word
θ-role	:	Thematic Role
R-expression	:	Referents
ROA	:	Rutgers University Optimality Archive
SCB	:	Standard Colloquial Bangla
SHB	:	Sylheti Dialect of Bangla
Spec	:	Specifier
TB	:	Tripura Bangla
TRO	:	Trochee
UG	:	Universal Grammar
WLP	:	Weak Local Parsing
WSP	:	Weight-to-Stress-Principle

A. Phonology

1

Who is Afraid of Noakhali Bangla?

1.0 Introduction

The present paper is part of an intended comprehensive study of a descriptive account of the various aspects of the phonology of the many East Bengali dialects spoken in different parts of Tripura. A mixed form of these dialects is commonly termed as Tripura Bangla (henceforth TB). The findings consequent upon this study would be presumably capable of throwing lights on the problems faced by the students of Tripura learning English as a second language. Three main dialects selected for this study are a) Noakhali Bangla (henceforth NKB), Cumilla Bangla (henceforth CB) and Sylheti Bangla (henceforth SHB). The first one is spoken in the southern parts of the state; CB is spoken mainly in the west district while SHB is primarily used in the northern parts of Tripura. In the first phase of this bigger project I take up the phonology of NKB; and the relevant discussions thereof are laid out as follows.

As a point of departure in §2.0 I initiate the discussion on the phonology of NKB. §2.1 presents the consonants in NKB highlighting their systematic weakening vis-à-vis those of Standard Colloquial Bangla or SCB. §2.1.1 presents a detailed account of the SCB obstruents and §2.1.2 deals with the sonorants in SCB. §2.2 focuses on the obstruents in NKB. In §2.2.1 under Simplification I discuss the obligatory phenomenon of deaspiration of voiced aspirates in NKB. Redistribution in §2.2.2 deals with the loss of the feature [spr.gl] in cases of non-initial voiceless obstruents. §2.2.2.1 focuses on the constraint against licensing labiality word initially in combination with the feature [-voiced]. Restructuring in §2.2.3 studies fricativization of affricates while Combination of Factors in §2.2.4 concentrates on the optional realization of initial /ʃ/ as /h/ in NKB. The identity of h in NKB constitutes the main point of discussion in §2.2.4.1. §2.2.5 deals with the sonorants in NKB and in §2.2.6 the discussion is focused on the semivowels in both the dialects. This part of the research is winded up in §2.3 with a comparative summary of the consonants in SCB and NKB in tabular form.

§3.0 introduces the study of the vowels in SCB and NKB. §3.1 looks at the oral and nasal monophthongs in SCB. §3.2 along with its subsections 3.2.1 and 3.2.2 gives the picture of the monophthongs in NKB. In NKB vowel length is contrastive and this is dealt with in §3.3. Another interesting aspect of the phonology of this non-standard variety is its use of lexical tone discussed in §3.4. There are however certain grey areas where it is difficult to ascertain absolutely the contrastive nature of tone in NKB as is shown in §3.5 under Free Variants. §3.6 and its subsections take up the issue of phonemic status of diphthongs in the two dialects of Bangla under study. We come to the end of this part of the study in §3.7 with a comparative summary of the vowels in the two varieties of Bangla. Finally, §4.0 recapitulates the major findings of the work.

2.0 Phonology of NKB

Why does the NKB sound so different from SCB or any other variety of Bangla for that matter? It is a common experience of the people of the South District of Tripura (particlualy belonging to Belonia and Santir Bazar sub-divisions) that whenever they speak in and around Agartala, the passersby turn around and cast a look of askance and leave the place with a smile of derision. And more often than not the

NKB speakers are subjected to ridicule and caricature of their linguistic behavior by those who speak a different variety of Bangla.

Subjecting the speakers of non-standard variety of a language to ridicule and fun by the speakers of the standard or quasi-standard variety of that is a universal phenomenon and has been studied thread bare by sociolinguists. This is primarily driven by a sense of prestige value added to the standard variety. But in modern times, any variety of linguistic communication is treated as worth studying because of the latter's being a rule-governed system: unless the native speakers/ users share the rules of a communicative system (read language) no exchange of ideas or meaning is possible.

In what follows I undertake a descriptive-comparative study of NKB as spoken in Tripura, in particular its phonological and morphological features which are primarily responsible for making it appear exotic to non-NKB speakers. In course of the study the SCB functions as the standard, however. Theoretical issues which crop up time to time, aiming at advanced students of linguistics, have been kept to the minimum however.

2.1 Consonants in NKB: A study in systematic weakening

The consonants particularly the obstruents in NKB have undergone a major reduction and restructuring compared to those of SCB due to the phonological processes of weakening which affects a number of them. For analytical convenience, we split up weakening into four major types: simplification, redistribution, restructuring and combination of factors and discuss them accordingly.

2.1.1 Consonants in SCB: Obstruents

According to Chatterji (1928), Paul (1972), Bhattacharrya (1988/ 1999) and Dasgupta (2003) among others there are twenty nine consonantal sounds in SCB. Of these eight are unaspirated and eight aspirated stops, two unaspirated and two aspirated affricates, and six sonorants comprising three liquids /l r ɽ/ and three nasals /m n ŋ/. I represent the distribution of the entire contingent of obstruents in SCB in the following auto-segmental tree.

1.

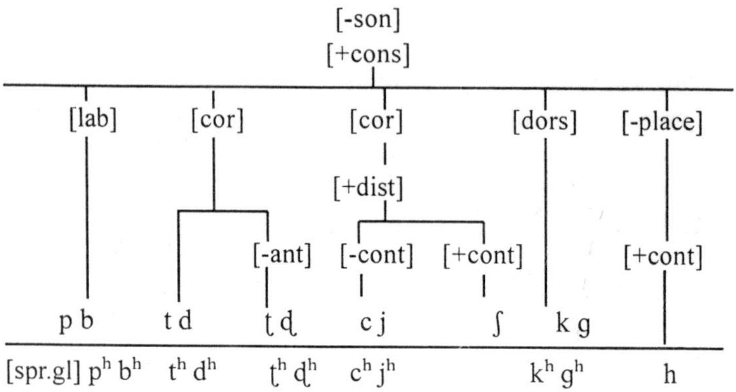

The obstruent inventory in SCB contains sixteen plosives (p p^h b b^h t t^h d d^h ʈ ʈ^{h}ɖ ɖ^h k k^h g g^h), four affricates (c c^h j j^h)[1] and two fricatives /ʃ, h/ as shown in (1). Contrary to Chatterji (1928) and also Paul (1972) I think it justified not to accord any phonemic status to [s] in this language. This is because, occurrence of [s] in SCB is predictably confined to the first position of a tautosyllabic consonant cluster. It never constitutes an onset or a coda all by itself. The second element of such a cluster can be a labial or a coronal or even a velar as we notice in (2) below.

2.	spɔrd^{h}a	'audacity'	slil	'decent'
	spɔndon	'mild vibration'	sneho	'affection'
	ɔsp^{h}uʈo	'indistinct'	ston	'breast'
	sp^{h}oʈik	'clear/transparent'	st^{h}ir	'static'
	srom	'labor'	skɔnd^{h}o[2]	'shoulder'
	srɔdd^{h}a	'respect'	sk^{h}ɔlon	'failure'

By contrast, the non-clustered counterpart of [s] i.e. the post-alveolar fricative /ʃ/ is not only capable of constituting an onset or coda independently, but also maintains its phonetic integrity even when preceded or followed by another consonant word medially as can be seen in (3).

3.	ʃap	'snake'	kutʃit	'ugly'
	ʃeʃ	'the end'	badʃa	'king'
	duʃkor	'difficult to accomplish'	bideʃ	'foreign'

Thus on the basis of its distributional limitation, its predictable occurrence and also 'phonetic similarity' to /ʃ/ we write off [s] as an allophonic variant of the former.

As for the plosives and affricates in SCB, given the fact that both voicing and aspiration are distinctive in the language, the entire list of plosive and affricate sounds can be sorted out into four contrastive sets as in (4).

4a.	A	B	C	D
	[-son]	[-son]	[-son]	[-son]
	[+cons]	[+cons]	[+cons]	[+cons]
	[-cont]	[-cont]	[-cont]	[-cont]
	[-voice]	[+voice]	[-voice]	[+voice]
			[spr.gl]	[spr.gl]
	/p t ʈ k/	/b d ɖ g/	/p^h t^h $ʈ^h$ k^h/	/b^h d^h $ɖ^h$ g^h/

4b.	A	B	C	D
	[-son]	[-son]	[-son]	[-son]
	[+cons]	[+cons]	[+cons]	[+cons]
	[-cont]	[-cont]	[-cont]	[-cont]
	[+dist]	[+dist]	[+dist]	[+dist]
	[-voice]	[+voice]	[-voice]	[+voice]
			[spr.gl]	[spr.gl]
	/c/	/j/	/c^h/	/j^h/

In addition to these plosives and affricates SCB has two fricatives /ʃ h/. The total number of obstruents in SCB therefore stands at twenty two.

2.1.2 Sonorants in SCB

As noted earlier SCB has six sonorants constituted of three liquids /l r ɽ/ and three nasals /m n ŋ/. There are however some distributional restrictions noted among these sonorants: e.g. /ɽ ŋ/ do not occur word initially; otherwise there is no constraint against their occurring in non-initial onsets as is shown by the data in (5).

5.

Liquids		Nasals	
/l/		/m/	
lal	'red'	mon	'mind'
alap	'discussion'	ami	'I'
dolil	'deed'	ɔʃim	'boundless'
/r/		/n/	
rani	'queen'	nodi	'river'
aram	'ease'	d^honi	'rich'
banor	'monkey'	proman	'evidence'
/ɽ/		/ŋ/	
aɽal	'obstacle'	aŋur	'graves'
aʃaɽ	'Bengali third month'	roŋ	'color'

2.2 Obstruents in NKB

Compared to SCB the obstruent inventory in NKB has undergone some drastic changes resulting in large scale reduction in the overall number of plosive sounds in particular. Whereas in SCB there are twenty [–cont], the number goes down to eleven in NKB. We identify the specific nature of these changes under four separate heads: Simplification, Redistribution, Restructuring and Combination of factors. Each of these processes merits close inspection with support from empirical evidence.

2.2.1 Simplification

The process of simplification affects the voiced aspirated stops and affricates most. The entire set of /b^h d^h $ɖ^h$ g^h/ and /j^h/ get deaspirated in all circumstances – initially, medially as well as finally[3]. Consequently they fall together with the corresponding voiced stops /b d ɖ g/ while j undergoes one more step of weakening heading towards fricativization. The sweeping generalization of the contexts of the application of simplification makes deaspiration of voiced aspirates an obligatory rule in NKB. In fact, as we shall see shortly, deaspiration affects even voiceless aspirates excepting in initial positions. The following examples from SCB and NKB bear this out.

	SCB	NKB		
6a.	b^hab	bab		'affection'
	ʃɔb^hab	ʃɔbab		'nature'
	d^han	dan		'paddy'
	bid^han	bidan		'decision'
	$ɖ^h$ol	ɖol		'drum'
	ɔ$ɖ^h$el	ɔɖel		'abundant'
	g^hum	gum		'sleep'
	ag^hat	agat		'injury'
6b.	j^hol	jol	⟶ [zol][4]	'gravy'
	maj^he	maje	⟶ [maze]	'in the middle'

The absence of any instance of word-final deaspiration in the data in (6) may lead one to question the validity of our observation that deaspiration of voiced aspirates is a rampant process in NKB. To dispel any misconceptions in this regard, one should take note of the fact that word final deaspiration is a regular phenomenon in SCB itself. Hence any contrast involving aspiration in such position is neutralized both in SCB as well as in NKB. The following examples will make the point clear.

7.	SCB				
	dud^h	[dud]	'milk'	[dud^he]	'in milk'
	maj^h	[maj]	'middle'	[maj^he]	'in the middle'
8.	NKB				
	?/dud^h/	[dud]	'milk'	[dude]	'in milk'
	maj	[maj]	'middle'	[maje]	'in the middle'

The surfacing of aspiration in the derived forms in right column in (7-8) is indicative of the fact that aspiration is present underlyingly even in the non-derived stems, although it is not phonetically realized word finally. By contrast the absence of aspiration is evident both in the derived and non-derived forms i.e. word medially and word finally in (8), although the contexts are quite identical as to those of (7). In other words, whereas in NKB deaspiration is an obligatory 'every where' rule, in SCB it is marginally effective – its application being predictably confined to the word final environment alone. So contrary to SCB any segment with the feature specifications [+voice, spr.gl] is not recorded in the underlying inventory in NKB.

2.2.2 Redistribution

Deaspiration or loss of the feature [spr.gl] from the feature metrics of non-continuant obstruents in NKB also affects the voiceless obstruents. Non-initial /p^h t^h ʈ^h k^h/ and /c^h/ neutralize to /p t ʈ k/ and /c/ respectively and thus fall together with the already existing set of corresponding sounds with the feature specification [-son, +cons, -voice]. Interestingly, deaspiration does not affect such obstruents word initially, with the exception of /p p^h/. These observations can be verified with the following data.

	SCB	NKB			
9a.	SCB	NKB			
	tup^{h}an	tupan[5] ~		[tuan]	'storm'
	dɔp^{h}a	dɔpa			'fold'
	mat^{h}a	mata			'head'
	kãʈ^{h}al	*kãʈɔl[6]	⟶	[kãɖɔl]	'jackfruit'
	boiʈ^{h}a	*boiʈa	⟶	[boiɖa]	'oar'
	rak^{h}al	rakal			'shepherd'
	pak^{h}a	*paka	⟶	[haka][7]	'fan'
9b.	ac^{h}aɽ	*acar	⟶	[asar]	'stumbling'
	goc^{h}a	*goca	⟶	[gosa]	'bunch'

10.

SCB	NKB		
p^halgun	halgun		'month of Phalgun'
p^hul	hul		'flower'
t^hana	t^hana		'police station'
t^hala	t^hal		'plate'
$ʈ^h$ik	$ʈ^h$ik		'right'
$ʈ^h$akur	$ʈ^h$akur ⟶	[$ʈ^h$aur]	'god'
k^hali	k^hali		'empty'
k^hur	k^hur		'razor'

The data in (9) exemplify non-initial deaspiration of voiceless plosives and affricates in NKB. Those in (10) on the other hand present empirical support to the claim that deaspiration does not affect such obstruents word initially except /p p^h/.

2.2.2.1 p, $p^h \rightarrow$h / #___

The above mentioned rule operating in NKB means voiceless labials in NKB are obligatorily realized as [h]. On closer inspection the core of the problem seems to lie, not so much in the presence of [h] but in the absence of accompanying place feature [lab] word initially for voiceless obstruents. This is because, in terms of Autosegmental Phonology, the feature [spr.gl] which universally represents aspiration, can be phonetically realized only as [h] in case the accompanying root node i.e. [-son, +cons] is unmarked for place. And in NKB there seems to be a particular constraint against licensing the feature [lab] in combination with [-voice] in the word initial position. This is attested by the following NKB examples.

11.

SCB	NKB		SCB	NKB	
pagol	hagɔl	'mad'	p^hɔl	hɔl	'fruit'
pagɽi	hagri	'head gear'	p^haltu	haltu	'trivial'
ponɖit	honɖit	'pundit'	p^hul	hul	'flower'
poribar	horibar	'family'	p^hæna	hæna	'foam'

An autosegmental account of the phenomenon can be formalized in terms of the following.

12. # [-son, +cons, -voice]
ǂ
[lab]

symbolizes word boundary on the left i.e. the word initial position and the Rule in (12) is specific only to this environment in NKB. In addition, we assume that this underspecified root node [-son, +cons, -voice] that emerges in consequence of delinking of the place feature [lab] remains so until the phonetic implementation module (or PIM) of the grammar (cf. PF or Phonetic Form) where it is realized as [h]. Notice, [h] is the prototypical segment unmarked for any place feature.

2.2.3 Restructuring

In the two preceding sections one must have noticed that there is no example showing the non-application of deaspiration to word initial voiceless affricates in NKB. Similarly, it should have been noted that the data in (9b) contain intermediate steps like *[acar] and *[goca] with non-initial deaspiration of voiceless affricates. In reality, the correct forms emerge with [s] in place of [c] i.e. an alveolar fricative in place of a palato-alveolar affricate. The same things happen to word initial affricates too (cf. 13).

13.

SCB	NKB	
c^hana	sana	'cheese'
chagol	sagɔl	'goat'
chobi	sobi	'picture'
chad	sad	'roof'

This, therefore, appears to contradict our claim that word initial voiceless aspirates are exempt from deaspiration. At the descriptive level, the answer to the problem lies in the fact that, in NKB all SCB affricates – both aspirated and unaspirated – neutralize to alveolar fricatives. Thus /c c^h/ become [s] and /j j^h/ are realized as [z], with the distinction maintained only in terms of voicing. This is an all-pervasive rule in the language and applies obligatorily independent of any contextual specification. The following examples are cited in support of this.

14a.	SCB	NKB	
	cakor	sakɔr	'servant'
	nice	nise	'below'
	bicar	bisar	'judgment'
14b.	SCB	NKB	
	c^{h}ãc	sãs	'dice'
	bic^{h}ana	bisana/bisna	'bed'
	mac^{h}	mas	'fish'
15a.	SCB	NKB	
	jamai	zamai	'son-in-law'
	jɔl	zɔl	'water'
	b^{h}ojɔn	bozɔn	'feast/eating'
	raja	raza	'king'
	kaj	kaz	'work'
	bij	biz	'seed'
15b.	SCB	NKB	
	j^{h}amela	zamæla	'chaos'
	j^{h}ɔgɽa	zɔgra	'quarrel'
	boj^{h}a	boza[8]	'burden'
	maj^{h}i	mazi	'boatman'

Word final deaspiration of voiced obstruents is a common process both in SCB and NKB (cf. 7-8). Hence no distinction is noticed between the two languages involving word final voiced aspirates.

But for a more principled account of the phenomenon it will not be incorrect to say that fricatives are redundantly [spr.gl], as attested by evidence from across languages. Harris (1969, 1985), for example, in course of his studies of the consonant weakening processes in Spanish, has provided ample evidence in support of this observation. Similarly, Vijaykrishnan (1993) discussing the phenomenon of dissimilation in Meitei Monipuri, talks of regular patterning between aspirates and fricatives. To be more specific, he notices that in this language, the presence of aspirates or fricatives in the root onset changes the suffixal aspirates or fricative onset to an unaspirated stop in one set of suffixes and the aspirate onset of another suffix to a voiced aspirate. These are strong evidence in favor of justifying [spr.gl] for fricatives in Meitei Monipuri.

On the basis of the above cross-linguistic facts we assume that in NKB too the fricatives /s z/ are redundantly specified for the feature [spr.gl] underlyingly. Thus the neutralization of SCB /c c^h/ and /j j^h/ to /s/ and /z/ respectively in NKB is not so much an evidence for loss of aspiration, as it is for restructuring i.e. the former set of obstruents is redefined as the latter, with the feature [spr.gl] remaining unhurt in the process, excepting that while it is non-redundantly marked in the former, in the latter it is redundantly specified.

2.2.4 Combination of Factors

It has already been noticed in §2.2.1 and §2.2.2 that deaspiration of SCB aspirated stops and fricatives is a rampant process in NKB, excepting when the segment is a word initial one with the feature specification [-voiced]. In addition, we have also noted in §2.2.2.1 that the place feature [lab] is not licensed word initially unless in combination with [+voiced] in NKB. Both these factors thus militate against according [p^h] the status of a separate phoneme in NKB. Hence [p^h] is not a part of the underlying phonemic alphabet of NKB. The realization of [p^h] as [h] in word initial position is taken care of by the phonetic implementation module.

In a similar process, word initial /ʃ/ is replaced by /h/ in NKB. But since this is an optional rule it allows free variants as the following examples show.

16. ʃuta	~	huta	'thread'	ʃag	~	hag	'vegetable leaves'
ʃala	~	hala	'brother-in-law	ʃali	~	hali	'sister-in-law'
ʃɔbe	~	hɔbe	'just now'	ʃidɔl	~	hidɔl	'kind of dry fish'
ʃɔkɔl	~	hɔgɔl	'all'	ʃun	~	hun	'to listen'

Both the options are equally exercised. However, in terms of non-linear phonology we split up the replacement process into a two-stage activity: delinking of features followed by filling-in by other feature values at the phonetic level. We represent the first stage as in (17).

17. [-son, +cor, -voice]
ǂ
[cor]
|
[+dist]
|
[+cont]

In the second stage the empty root node is filled in by some feature values which are phonetically realized as [h] – the typical segment marked as [-place]. Since the second stage takes place at the phonetic implementation module, it needs not detain us any more. Significantly, there are many counter examples to the /ʃ/ ~ [h] alternation in NKB and the following examples amply reflect this restrictiveness.

18.	ʃal	~	*hal	'shawl'
	ʃazna	~	*hazna	'drumstick'
	ʃagɔr	~	*hagɔr	'sea'
	ʃanti	~	*hanti	'peace'
	ʃari	~	*hari	'sari'

Such examples provide a stronger support in favour of the optional status of the rule of /ʃ/ ~ [h] alternation in NKB. Such optionality must have serious implications for phonological theory.

2.2.4.1 Identity of [h] in NKB

Before we wind up the issue of NKB obstruents a logical question crops up as to what is the underlying identity of [h] in the language particularly given the fact that a number of obstruents, i.e. both plosives and fricatives, weaken to [h]. To be more specific 'What happens to the SCB /h/ in NKB?' and 'How does the SCB /h/ behave with respect to the 'derived' one in NKB?'

Descriptively, the answer is that the original SCB /h/ is lost in NKB and it is a context-free rule that applies obligatorily as is testified by the following.

19.	SCB	NKB		SCB	NKB	
	hat	at	'hand'	hata	ata	'handle'
	hal	al	'plough'	hati	ati	'elephant'
	holud	olud	'yellow'	mɔhan	mɔan	'great'
	haʃi	ãʃi	'laughter'	loha	loa	'iron'

No word in SCB ends in /h/. So no instance of word final /h/ deletion is noticed in NKB. This we assume to redundantly support our claim that /h/ deletion is a ubiquitous phenomenon in NKB. The [h] that one comes across in NKB, is not identical to SCB /h/ and therefore should not give rise to any confusion. Instead, as has been already done, the NKB [h] should be interpreted as a consequence of a 'fill-in' at phonetic implementation module[9] of the grammar so that the underspecified root node could be pronounceable. Hence, we conclude that [h] in NKB is not a part of the underlying phoneme list of the language and the derived [h] gets its features only from PIM.

To sum up, we have noticed that

a) the entire set of voiced aspirates is lost in NKB;

b) /pʰ/ should not be treated as part of the underlying inventory of the language, because although /pʰ/ exists in principle it is never phonetically realized: it is neutralized to [h] word initially and to [p] elsewhere.

c) /p pʰ/ and optionally /ʃ/ weaken to [h] with the result that [h] is only a derived segment in NKB with no existence in the underlying inventory; and

d) finally, that the SCB affricates /c cʰ/ and /j jʰ/ get fricativized to /s/ and /z/ respectively.

The cumulative effects of these changes in NKB result in an over all reduction of the total number of obstruents: as opposed to sixteen stops and four affricates in SCB, NKB has only eleven stops and no affricates at all as shown in (20).

20.	A	B	C
	[-son]	[-son]	[-son]
	[+cons]	[+cons]	[+cons]
	[-voice]	[+voice]	[-voice]
			[spr. gl]
	/p t ʈ k/	/b d ɖ g/	/tʰ ʈʰ kʰ/

Additionally, two new fricatives /s/ and /z/ have been introduced in NKB with the result that NKB has three fricatives /s z ʃ/ while the SCB list of fricatives contains only two /ʃ h/. [h] is not a part of the underlying list of obstruents in NKB: at the most it is a derived segment emerging at the surface or PF. The number of obstruents in NKB therefore stands at fourteen as opposed to SCB twenty two. The following diagram gives a neat picture of the distribution of NKB obstruents.

21.

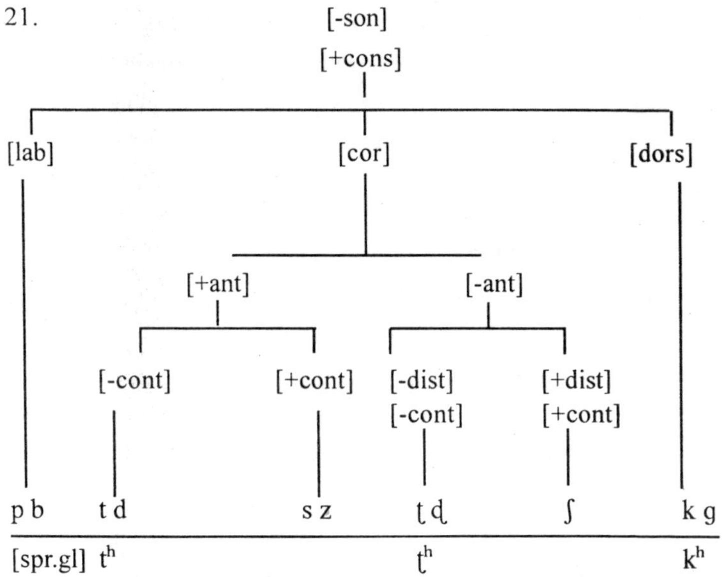

2.2.5 Sonorants in NKB

In §2.1.1 we have seen that SCB has six sonorants divided into two groups: liquids /l r ɽ/ and nasals /m n ŋ/. Besides, it has also been noticed that there are some distributional asymmetries noted among these sonorants: e.g. /ɽ ŋ/ do not occur word initially; these consonants can however occur in non-initial onsets (cf. 5).

Compared to SCB, NKB shows some marked 'deviations'. For instance, a) [ɽ] does not exist in NKB; and b) [ŋ] occurs only in the syllable coda whether final or not. The distributional pattern of the NKB sonorants is shown below with the same set of examples used for SCB in (5) above with the NKB version of the 'changed' segments. This will make the segmental distinction between the two dialects quite clear.

22. Liquids Nasals

/l/		/m/	
lal	'red'	mɔn	'mind'

alap	'discussion'	ami	'I'
dolil	'deed'	oʃim	'boundless'
/r/		/n/	
rani	'queen'	nodi	'river'
aram	'ease'	doni	'rich'
bandɔr	'monkey'	prɔman	'evidence'
/ɽ/		/ŋ/	
aral	'obstacle'	aŋgur	'graves'
aʃar	'Bengali third month'	rɔŋ[10]	'color'

Since there is no difference between [ɽ] and [r] in NKB, both sound like the latter.

2.2.6 Semi-vowels

Talking about the presence of semivowels in SCB, Dasgupta (2003) writes:

> Any account of intervocalic glides must note the unavailability of semivowel onsets. Items like /yār/ 'mate', /yārki/ 'jest', /wāriš/ 'heir', /wār/ 'pillow-case' can be pronounced with initial semivowels. But most speakers and all writers substitute /i(y)ā/, /o(w)ā/, *i(y)ā*, *oyā*. We conclude that intervocalic semivowels count as interludes. The language has no true onset semivowels. (p. 356).

These intervocalic interludes or intrusives are either of y-type or w-type: the former are contiguous to /i, e/ and the latter next to /u, o/. Significantly their use is 'consistently optional': di(y)o 'give, Imp. Fut.', je(y)o 'go, Imp. Fut.' halu(w)a 'semolina dish', ʃo(w)a 'to lie down' etc. [for details one is referred to (ibid)].

In Das (1996), I have argued with ample empirical support that in NKB also the semivowels y and w as onsets do not exist in the true sense of the term. SCB forms, optional by themselves, like /dud^{h}o (w)ala/ is pronounced as /dudɔla/ or /dudala/ 'milkman', daɽio(w)ala as /dariala/ or dariɔla 'bearded man'. Again Sanskrit (originated) words like /yamini/ 'night' and /yɔm/ 'Yom, the god of death' are pronounced as /zamini/ and /zɔm/ respectively. Moreover, among the SCB words noted above in Dasgupta (2003) /yār/ 'mate', /yārki/ 'jest', /wāriš/ 'heir', /wār/ 'pillow-case' the first and last one do not exist in NKB. As for /yārki/ and /wāriš/ as Dasgupta (ibid) rightly points out, the Bangla speakers whether of SCB or NKB visualize the two as [iarki] and [oariʃ] respectively. The emergence of *y* in between i & a and *w* between o & a is more of a phonetic than a phonological phenomenon.

2.3 A Comparative Summary of the Consonants in SCB and NKB

To conclude our study of the consonants in NKB, we present here a consonant chart of the non-standard variety (24) preceded by one presented for the standard dialect in (23).

23. **SCB consonants**

		Labial	De-ntal	Alve olar	Retro flex	Alveo-Palatal	Velar	Glo ttal
		Vl Vd	Vl Vd	Vd	Vl Vd	Vl Vd	Vl Vd	Vl
Plosive	Un-asp	p b	t d		ʈ ɖ		k g	
	Asp	p^h b^h	t^h d^h		ʈ^h ɖ^h		k^h g^h	
Fricative						ʃ		h
Affricate	Asp					c j		
	Un-asp					c^h j^h		
Nasal		m		n			ŋ	
Flap				r		ɽ		
Lateral				l				

24. NKB Consonants

		Labial	Dental	Alveo-lar	Retro flex	Alveo-Palatal	Velar
		Vl Vd	Vl Vd	Vl Vd	Vl Vd	Vl Vd	Vl Vd
Plosive	Un-asp	p b	t d		ʈ ɖ		k g
	Asp		t^h		$ʈ^h$		k^h
Fricative				s z		ʃ	
Nasal		m		n			ŋ
Flap				r			
Lateral				l			

3.0 Vowels in SCB and NKB

After having paid attention in detail to the non-vocalic segmental phonology in NKB we now turn to the vowel phonology of the dialect. For this it would be sensible once again to adopt a comparative approach. SCB once again is taken as the model. As we shall see before long, the vowels in both these dialects of Bangla use additional dimensions like length, nasality, and even tone to ensure perceptual distinctions amongst themselves. To begin with, we look at the SCB picture.

3.1 SCB Monophthongs: Oral and nasal — /i e æ a ɔ o u/ and /ĩ ẽ æ̃ ã ɔ̃ õ ũ/

For a clear picture of the locational positions of the SCB monophthongs both oral and nasal (nasality is distinctive in the language) let us look at the following diagram.

25.

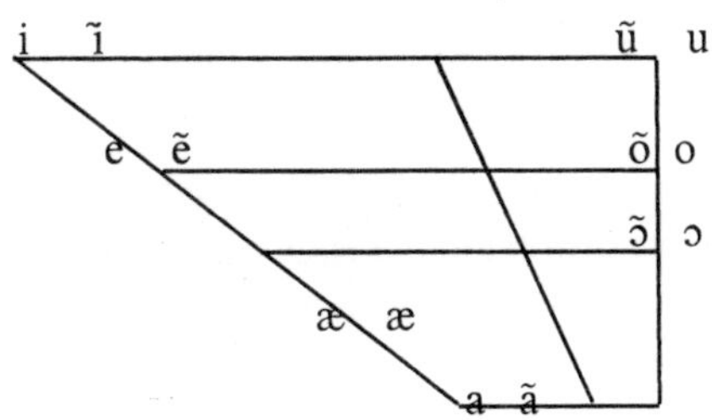

The above picture of the vowel zone utilization by SCB is based on Bhattacharya (1988/1999) which finds support also from Chakraborty (2006) and Dasgupta (2003), among others. Dasgupta (ibid) however does not directly address the issue of nasal vowels. As per this picture, there are seven oral monophthongs in SCB /i e æ a ɔ o u/ and their contrastive nasal counterparts. We show the distribution of the oral ones in (26) and the nasal ones in (27) below.

	Initial		Medial		Final	
26a. /i/	iliʃ	'hilsha fish'	biʃal	'large'	biɽi	'country cigar'
	itihaʃ	'history'	hiŋʃa	'hatred'	kaʃi	'cough'
26b. /e/	elem	'capacity'	bel	'wood apple'	mej^{h}e	'floor'
	emon	'like this'	tel	'oil'	meʈe	'lever'
26c. /æ/	æk	'one'	dæk	'see IMP, Non-hon'	—	
	æka	'alone'	mæla	'fair'	—	
26d. /a/	alu	'potato'	kal	'time'	kala	'deaf'
	agun	'fire'	kali	'ink'	pata	'leaf'
26e. /ɔ/	ɔloʃ	'idle'	kɔloʃ	'pitcher'	ʃɔhɔ	'with'
	ɔlpo	'a little'	bɔl	'energy'		
26f. /o/	ozon	'weight'	gola	'granary'	ʃolo	'sixteen'
	oj^{h}a	'sorcerer'	tola	'lift'	maŋʃo	'meat'
26g. /u/	udar	'generous'	putul	'doll'	alu	'potato'
	uʃa	'dawn'	agun	'fire'	aʃu	'immediate'

Unlike the oral monophthongs in SCB the nasal monophthongs display a rather restrictive distribution. Beside the fact that the latter occurs in a very limited number of lexical items, their occurrence in the final position is extremely restricted. The nasal vowels are never attested in the final syllable of a word having more than one syllable.

No examples could be found even in open monosyllabic words for /ĩ ẽ æ̃ ɔ̃/. We refrain from showing examples of phonetic nasalization of vowel preceding a nasal consonant in the data, since they do not have any implication for the phonological status of the underlying vowel inventory of NKB.

	Initial		Medial		Final	
27a. /ĩ/	ĩdur	'rat'	pĩaj	'onion'	—	
	ĩʈ	'brick'	ʃĩɽi	'flights'		
27b./ẽ/	ẽʈo	'orts'	k^{h}ẽk	'yelp of dog'	—	
	ẽʈuli	'lick'	pẽpe	'papaw'		
27c. /æ̃/	æ̃ɽ	'testicles'	gæ̃ɽa	'dwarf'	—	
	æ̃c^{h}oɽ	'tender jackfruit'	c^{h}æ̃k	'searing'		
27d. /ã/	ãʈi	'bundle'	k^{h}ãʈi	'pure'	bã	'left'
	ãʃ	'fiber of a tree'	bãʃi	'flute'	gã	'village'
27e. /ɔ̃/	—		pɔ̃ca	'rotten' knife'	—	
				bɔ̃ʈi	'fish-	
27f. /õ/	õra	'they, Hon'	gõja	'insert'	gõ	'obstinacy'
	õke	'him, Hon.'	d^{h}õka	'deception'	b^{h}õ	'trumpet sound'
27g. /ũ/	ũcu	'high'	k^{h}ũt	'fault'	p^{h}u	'puff of breath'
	ũki	'peeping'	ʈ^{h}ũʈo	'disabled'	ɖ^{h}ũ	'a butt'

3.2 NKB Monophthongs

Now we turn to NKB pure vowels. Compared to the standard

dialect the NKB has one vowel short: i.e. the vowel [e] is absent in the non-standard dialect. The distribution of these six vowels in the vowel zone is shown in (28) followed by empirical support in (29).

3.2.1 Orals in NKB: /i æ a ɔ o u/

28.

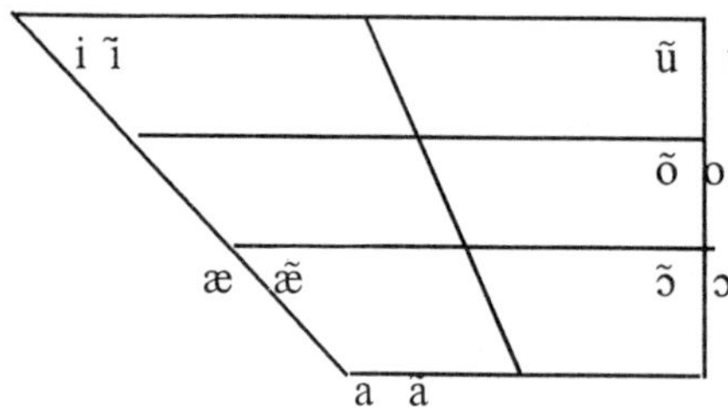

29a. /i/

Initial		Medial		Final	
itɔr	'rascal'	diʃa	'sense'	siɖi	'letter'.
iliʃ	'hilsa fish'	biɖal	'crooked'	ali	'unit of four'
iʃab	'account'	bisi	'seed'	maɖi	'mud/earth',

29b. /æ/

æk	'one'	bæk	'all'	—	
ær	'put/keep'	dæʃ	'country'		
ræn	'look IMP, non-hon'	adæʃ	'order'		
læʃ	'trace'	biʃæʃ	'special'		

29c. /a/

aʈ	'eight'	kaʈ	'wood'	aʈa	'flour'
at	'hand'	bat	'arthritis'	kãɖa	'thorn'
ata	'handle /big spoon'	kal	'danger'	miɖa	'molasses'

29d. /ɔ/

ɔʃɔt	'wicked'	nɔrɔm	'soft'	soʈʈɔ	'small'
ɔlɔʃ	'idle'	bɔl	'energy'	kʰɔrɔ	'sour'
ɔlpɔ	'a little'	ʃikɔr	'root'	barɔ	'twelve'

29e. /o/

oza	'sorcerer'	hola	'son/boy'	bo	'bride'
ozɔn	'heavy'	gola	'granary'	tʰo	'put IMP, Non-hon'
oda	'wet/damp'	sor	'thief'	do	'wash IMP, non-hon'

29f. /u/

uɖa	'act of rising'	uruʃ	'bug'	ãɖu	'knee'
udam	'bare'	baluʃ	'pillow'	balu	'sand'
usit	'just'	sul	'hair'	zamu	'go 1FUT'
udar	'lending'	mur	'deep'	alu	'potato'

3.2.2 Nasal monophthongs in NKB: /ĩ æ̃ ã ɔ̃ õ ũ/

All the vowels with the tilde ˜ on their head in the vowel diagram in (28) represent the nasal counterparts of the oral vowels examined in (29) above. That nasality is contrastive in SCB has already been noted in (27) vis-à-vis (26). In both the dialects nasalization of the vowel can be both phonetic and phonological. Phonetic nasalization is the consequence of the spreading of the feature [nasal] from a following nasal consonant to the preceding vowel followed by subsequent deletion of trigger i.e. the nasal consonant as in sequences like kʰan → kʰã 'surname', ami → ãi 'I', tumi →tũi 'you' etc. The process in NKB however is not an all pervasive one: kamar → *kãr blacksmith, tæna → *tæ̃a 'rug' , anarɔʃ → *ãrɔʃ etc. The theoretical explanation for such eclectic application of the 'pinapple' rule of nasalization is however not the concern of the present study and hence awaits further study. Instead, we confine our scope of investigation to the descriptive survey of the phenomenon in the non-standard dialect as opposed to the standard one. The phonological nasal vowels in NKB are instantiated in the following data in (30).

30a. /ĩ /

ĩʈ 'brick'		sĩɖa	'dead paddy'	hĩ	'drink up'
ĩs 'bail-out water'		sĩsa	'slanting rainfall'	sĩsĩ	'chirping'
ĩɖa 'stone-throw'		hĩsa	'broom'	kĩkĩ	'metal sound'
ĩsa 'shrimp'		hĩsla	'slippery'		

30b. /æ̃/

æ̃ 'expression of surprise'		k^hæ̃s	'beat/thrash'	—
æ̃tɔ	'like this'	bæ̃ra	'ram'	
æ̃ska	'sudden pull'	hæ̃sa	'owl'	
hæ̃za	'porcupine'			

30c. /ã/

ãska	'suddenly'	dãri	'beard'	sã	'tea'
ãr	'my'	gãri	'car/bus'	bã	'left'
ãti	'elephant'	bãʃ	'bamboo'	gã	'add flavour'
ãtur	'crippled'	bãʃi	'flute'	kã-kã	'hue and cry'

30d. /ɔ̃/

—	hɔ̃t	'path'	gɔ̃	'urge/desire'
	bɔ̃t	'bass sound'		
	gɔ̃t	'routine'		

30e. /õ/

õʃ	'commonsense'	hõza	'burden'	sõ	'suck, IMP'
õsa	'high'	ʃõza	'straight'	kõ	'groan'
õra	'basket'	sõt	'quick'	hõ	'to smell'
õtla	'quagmire'	hõs	'wipe IMP'	ʃõ-ʃõ	'sound of storm'

30f. /ũ/

ũʈ	'camel'	hũri	'dry fish'	kʰũ	'to open'
ũkki	'peeping'	hũz	'puss'	hũ	'puff of breath'

Just like the phenomenon in case of SCB nasal monophthongs, the NKB nasal vowels also display a very restrictive distributional pattern. The vowel /ɔ̃/ is not attested in the word initial position; and in the final position the picture is in no way better: /gɔ̃/ 'urge/desire' being the only word available in this respect. The other vowel disallowed in the word final position is /æ̃/. It is the general characteristic of NKB that very few underived lexical items end in a vowel whether nasal or non-nasal. In the derived context it is primarily the inflexional suffixes that render, through resyllabification, the final syllable an open one: e.g. hat 'hand, Nom. Sg.', hat-e 'hand, Loc. Sg.', ka:ʈ 'cut, Imp.'→ kaɖe[11] 'cut, 3. Prs. Ind.' etc.

3.3 Contrastive Vowel length in NKB

In having both nasal and non-nasal monophthongs both SCB and NKB show parity. But in the non-standard dialect we observe an additional dimension enforcing contrastive relationship among vowels namely vowel length. In (31) below I present the relevant data which are rather exhaustive.

31a. /i/~ /i:/	bir	'hero'	bi:r	'tighten'
	hiʈ	'back'	hi:ʈ	'beat Imp.'
	hin	'wear, Imp.'	hi:n	'phlegm'

31b. /æ/~/æ:/	bæk	'pretence'	bæ:k	'all'
	bæl	'wood apple'	bæ:l	'roll. Imp.'
	mæl	'assembly'	mæ:l	'spread Imp.'
	dær	'one and half'	dæ:r	'see, 3 Prs. Prog'
	hæn	'rice froth'	hæ:n	'pant'
	bæʃ	'excess'	bæ:ʃ	'dress'
31c. /a/ ~/a:/	maz	'middle'	ma:z	'rub, Imp'
	nas	'dance'	na:s	'dance Imp'
	gas	'tree'	ga:s	'sing, 2 Prs.Hab.'
	zal	'net'	za:l	'sister-in-law'
	gal	'cheek'	ga:l	'press out the liquid from'
	ga	'body'	ga:	'sing, Imp'
	kaʈ	'wood'	ka:ʈ	'cut, Imp'
	bãʃ	'bamboo'	bã:ʃ	'foul smell'
	ban	'tie'	ba:n	'hue and cry'
	al	'sting'	a:l	'plough'
	ãʃ	'fiber'	ã:ʃ	'duck'
31d. /ɔ/~ /ɔ:/	kɔ	'Bangla 'k'	kɔ:	'speak Imp.'
	kɔn	'who'	kɔ:n	'when/speak Imp'
	hɔr	'stranger'	hɔ:r	'dawn'/to forget'
	bɔn	'forest'	bɔ:n	'sit, Imp'
	sɔl	'let us go'	sɔ:l	'harpoon to kill fish etc'

	sɔr	'beach'	sɔ:r	'see/want, 2 Prog'
	hɔ̃t	'path'	hɔ̃:t	'horn'
	k^{h}ɔr	'hideout of fish'	k^{h}ɔ:r	'eat, 2 Prog'
	bɔra	'kind of snacks'	bɔ:ra	'deaf'
31e. /o/~/o:/	sok	'eye'	so:k	'let somebody till the land'
	gol	'round'	go:l	'goal'
	kol	'lap'	ko:l	'whirlpool'
	lok	'man/ people'	lo:k	'let somebody take'
	t^{h}or	'plant- ain flower'	t^{h}o:r	'keep3.Prs. Prog'
	sor	'thief'	so:r	'of eye'
	mos	'mou- stache'	mo:s	'wipe, Imp.'
31f. /u/~/u:/	guna	'iron wire'	gu:na	'sin'
	gum	'conceal'	gu:m	'sleep'
	muri	'perched rice'	mu:ri	'deed writer'
	huna	'heard'	hu:na	'dry'
	gũra	'dust/children'	gũ:ra	'cricket (insect)'
	rui	'plant,1. PRS'	ru:i	'kind of fish'

3.4 Lexical tone in NKB

An interesting phenomenon comes up in course of the present study namely the presence of lexical tone in NKB. It has been observed that the entire series of obstruents having the combination [+spr.gl, +voice] is lost in NKB. Additionally, among the obstruents, those with the featural combination of [-voice, +spr.gl], are retained only in the word initial syllable onset. In other places it becomes either simply [-spr.gl] as in mat^{h}a → mata 'head', $\text{kɔt}^{h}\text{a}$ → kɔta 'speech' or the segment undergoes voicing following deaspiration as in $\text{aʈ}^{h}\text{a}$ → aɖa 'glue'. It is noted that wherever the feature [+spr.gl] is lost in NKB, there emerges a tonal substitute in the form of a Rising or High tone represented here by the sign ['] put on the consonant concerned or the nucleus of the syllable when the aspirate consonant is either lost as in /a't/ < SCB /hat/ 'hand' or the onset of the second syllable in SCB is an aspirate as in /a'sar/ < SCB /$\text{a.c}^{h}\text{aɽ}$/ 'stumbling'. Significantly, no tone is substituted for the deaspiration of a coda consonant whether word-final or not. This is probably because in the coda all aspirates undergo deaspiration even in SCB (cf. 32).

32. SCB

Orthographic	Phonetic	Derived Adjective/Noun	
mach 'fish'	[mac]	mac + o = mec^{h}o	'of or like fish'
dudh 'milk'	[dud]	dud + al = dud^{h}al	'milking (cow etc.)'
majh 'middle'	[maj]	maj + e = maj^{h}e	'in the middle'
laph 'jump'	[lap]	lap + ano = lap^{h}ano	'jumping'

(33) provides the relevant examples of words with deaspirated onsets accompanied by a High tone as compensation.

33.

Low/Level Tone		**High Tone Tone**		**Low/Level Tone**		**High Tone**	
sal	'thatch'	s'al	'hide/skin'	ada	'ginger'	a'da	'half'
san	'moon'	s'an	'bathing'	gadi	'heap'	g'adi	'she donkey'

sak	'rock of earth'	s'ak	'filtrate,' Imp.	biri	'raw cigarette'	b'iri	tighten '1prs'
haʈ	'jute'	h'aʈ	'to burst'	bari	'house'	b'ari	'heavy'
hal	'to rear'	h'al	'jump'	bori	'tablet'	b'ori	'gold unit'
zal	'net'	z'al	'hot'	baɖi	'small bowl'	b'aɖi	'low ebb'
zama	'shirt'	z'ama	'rock stone'	dara	'stand Imp.'	d'ara	'flow'
zala	'sapling'	z'ala	'welding'	dari	'beard'	d'ari	'bamboo mat'
sala	'behavior'	s'ala	'gunny bag'	ɖula	'fish basket'	ɖ'ula	'jolt, Imp.'
mata	'mother'	m'ata	'head'	ɖala	'flat basket'	ɖ'ala	'pouring'
asar	'pickle'	a'sar	'stumbling'	siɖa	'essen-celess'	s'iɖa	'spread, Imp.'
agat	'at the top'	a'gat	'injury'	sira	'flat rice'	s'ira	'torn'
apɔd	'danger'	a'pɔd	'rascal'	bilai	'cat'	b'ilai	'Bhilai'
adar	'of ginger'	a'dar	'fish feed'	baʃa	'home'	b'aʃa	'language'
baŋgi	'kind of fruit'	b'aŋgi	'I break'	bari	'home'	b'ari	'heavy'
baza	'play, Imp.'	b'aza	'fried'	hoir	'pond'	h'oir	'beggar'
bas	'restric-tion'	b'a:s	'sort out'	hon	'rectum'	h'o:n	'phone/ pure'
sir	'slice'	s'i:r	'split, Imp.'	gun	'quality'	g'u:n	'termite'

gur	'mola-sses'	g'u:r	'turn around,'	dur	'distant'	d'u:r	'expression of disapproval'

3.5 Free variants among NKB vowels

In the examples in (33) the reason for tonogenesis is the loss of aspiration or the feature [spr.gl]. But on occasions even an underlying unaspirated consonant can be alternatively accompanied by a High tone. In such cases one also perceives a distinct lengthening of the syllable nuclei. It is examples like these that stand as counterexamples to the fact of vowel length being counted as signifying lexical contrast in NKB. The matter however requires threadbare investigation with instrumental aids.

34.	kɔr	'lines on palm'	~	k'ɔr	'do, Imp.'
	kan	'ear'	~	k'an	'weep, Imp.'
	kɔʃ	'juice of tree'	~	k'ɔʃ	'tighten, Imp.'
	kali	'(black) ink'	~	k'ali	'goddess Kali'
	k^hir	'juice of tree'	~	k^h'ir/.	'cheese'

3.6 Diphthongs in NKB and SCB

Discussion on diphthongs is usually out of fashion in serious theoretical discourse in phonology. But since our present concern is primarily descriptive, for a comprehensive picture of the distribution of diphthongs in the two dialects of Bangla it is desirable not to overlook this aspect of the vowel phonology in the two systems.

3.6.1 Oral Diphthongs in NKB

There are sixteen diphthongs having contrastive value in NKB. Some of these diphthongs allow nasalized forms either as separate phonemes, or free variants or simply as phonetic realizations when followed by a nasal consonant. These diphthongs are /ui, ei, ai, oi, au, eu, ia, ua, oa, ɔa, ea, ia, iɔ, ɛə, aɔ, oɔ, uɔ/ presented with examples as the following.

35a. /ui/

Initial		Medial		Final	
uit	'upside down'	ruit	'kind of fish'	t^hui	'keep, 1 Prs. Ind.'
uil	'pleader'	guilla	'iron in fishing net	s'ui	'touch, 1 Prs. Ind.'
		kuicca	'eel'	kui	'shrill voice'
		zuit	'comfort'	rui	'to plant sapling'
		uḍuilla	'refugee'	hui	'sleep 1Prs. Ind'

35b. /ei/

ei	'this'	ḍeila	'veranda'	hei	'that'
eicca	'like this'	keicca	'like what'	zei	'which'
eiḍa	'this one'	meicca	'leopard'	dei	'having seen'
eitan	'these things'	beiman	'ungrateful'	ḍei	'having jumped over'
eikkɔn	'just now'	beiṭṭa	'effeminate'		
eitori	'till now'	leit	'line/series'		
eito	'here/now'	teilla	'oily'		
		adeilla	'possessed by ill-luck'		

35c. /ai/

ailla	'help in husking'	b'aisa	'brother'	hanai	'musical instrument'
airga	'cross wise'	mairga	'disease'	gai	'cow'
ailʃa	'idle'	mair	'beat'	hitai	'devil god'
air	'kind of fish'	baila	'kind of fish'	nai	'not having'

ain 'law' baicca 'calf' b'ai 'brother'

ail 'border of paddyland' 'bough of tree' g'ai 'pierce'
ʈ^{h}aila

ailka 'middle of banana tree' 'caste' sai 'fishing trap'
zait ɖail 'pulse' lai 'bamboo basket'

b'ail 'proper order' zamai gõʃai 'priesthood' 'groom'

35d. /oi/

oi 'that'	s'oil	'cut off'	s'oi	'bean'
oiɖa 'that one'	koiɖa	'snake gourd'	koi	'kind of fish'
oiran 'excessive reaction'	boiragi	'religious beggar'	doi	'curd '
	boisa	'small fish'	moi	'ladder'

35e. /au/

aur 'cover'	t^{h}auga	'baseless/untrue'	lau	'gourd'
	bauʃ	'kind of fish'	zau	'starched rice'
	ʈ^{h}aur	'god/priest'	kau	'type of fruit'
	gaur	'labourer'	sau	'grinding machine'
			hau	'without cost'

35f. /eu/

—-	b'eura	'makeshift boat'	ɖeu	'wave'
	beula	'proper name'	g'eu	'barking'

35g. /ia/

—-		bial	'afternoon'	bia	'marriage'
				k'ia	'what'
				sia	'lean and thin
				ɓia	'hip'

35h /ua/

ua	'erect'	duar	'door'	kua	'pond'
uaʃ	'fast'	huar	'use'	t^hua	'put together'
		huak	'let it dry up'	sua	'sour'
				b'ua	'false'
				hua	'dry, Imp'

35i. /oa/

oa	'be/beget'	boal	'type of fish'	toa	'search'
oal	'wall'	koal	'dove'	d'oa	'washed/ washer man'
		goar	'bamboo to tie fence'	loa	'iron'
		ʃoar	'possessed by spirit'	s'oa	'touch'
		zoar	'flood'	z'oa	'festival'

35j. /ɔa/

		hɔad	'taste'	bɔa	'sit, causative '
ɔa	'expression of ' wonder	sɔar	'slap'	kɔa	'speak, causative'
		bɔar	'sit, 3 causative, Prg.'	lɔa	'take'
				nɔa	'new'

35k. /ea/

ea	'stopgap in speech'	bead	'wicked'	dea	'seeing'
		seara	'face'	lea	'writing'
		mead	'permissible time'		
		zead	'challenge'		

35l. /iɔ/

—-		ʃiɔr	'pillow'	attiɔ	'relative'
		siɔl	'chain'		
		biɔz'	'scurvy'		

35m. /ɛɔ/

—-		dɛɔr	'husband's younger brother	dɛɔ	'body'
		kɛɔr	'of nobody'	s'ɛɔ	'piece/ slice'
				kɛɔ	'no body'

35n. /aɔ/

—-		aɔn	'act of coming'	k^{h}aɔn	'food/eating'
		saɔn	'wanting/seeing'		

35o. /oɔ/

—-		roɔr	'plant, Caus. Prg.'	roɔ	'plant, Caus. Imp.'
		doɔr	'milk, 2, Prg'	doɔ	'milk, Caus, Imp'

35p. /uɔ/

uɔr	'exceed'	huɔr	'pig'	t^{h}uɔ	'put together, Imp'

3.6.2 Nasal dipththongs in NKB

Of the sixteen oral diphthongs in NKB exemplified in (35) there are nasal counterparts for the first twelve. Of the remaining four only one /oɔ/ has a nasal form in /õɔ̃/. There are thus only thirteen nasal vowels in NKB. The distributional patter is also not symmetrical between the oral and nasal diphthongs in the dialect. These facts are borne out in the data in (36).

36a. /ũĩ/

—	hũĩs	'needle'	tũĩ	'you'
	hũĩcca	'pointed'	k^hũĩ	'open/damage'
	ʈũĩnna	'petty'	mũĩ	'mother's sister'
	hũĩkka	'peep'	sũĩ	'suck 1 Prs. Ind'
	mũĩt	'roaming around'	hũi	'to smell'

36b. /ẽĩ/

ẽĩkka 'like this'	kẽĩkka/ kẽĩnna	'like what'	ɖ'ẽi	'wooden husking device'
	hẽĩcca	'type of bird'		

36c. /ãĩ/

ãi	'I'	hãĩnna	'water born'	hãĩ	'husband'
'ãĩʃ	'joy'	bãĩnna	'gold merchant'	dãĩ	'beard'
ãĩmma	'yawn, Imp.'	bãĩn	'design'	gãĩ	'car'
ãĩʃ	'scale of fish'	tãĩn	'3 Sg. Hon'		
		gain	'singer'		

36d. /õĩ/

—	bõĩt	'in the book'	gõĩ	'dry cow dung'
	bõĩʃ	'buffalo'	s'õĩ	'bean'
	mõĩs	'chilly'	bõĩ	'book'

gõĩnna	'kind of fish'	bõĩn	'sister'
mõĩna	'endearing term'		

36e. /ãũ/

ãũ 'walk on all four'	—-	kãũ kãũ 'make noise'

36f. /ẽũ/

—-	—-	kẽũ kẽũ 'expression of pain by a puppy or dog

36g. /ĩã/

ĩãn	'this one'	hĩãn	'that one'	bĩã	'deliver a baby'
		hĩãl	'jackal'	ɦĩã	'parrot'
		t^hĩãn	'wait, Imp. Hon'	zĩa	'put fish in water'
		mĩãn	'mix up, Imp. Hon.'	z'ĩã	'vegetable type'
				mĩã	Muslim male'

36h. /ũã/

—-		hũãʃ	'pipe to blow fire'		
			hũã	'blow, Imp.'	
		zũãl	'yoke'	mũã	'of or about mouth'
		d'ũãl	'enthusiasm'		

36i. /õã/

õã	'sound of weeping of small babies'	kõãni	'groaning'	kõã	'cell of jackfruit etc.
		gõãr	'adamant		
		õãr	to spoil by excessive praising'	gõã	'rectum'

	kõãr	'potter'	sõã	'twigs of bamboo'
	tõãr	'your'	s'õã	'touch'
	zõãn	'young'	n'õã	'bangle'
	dõãn	'shop'	hõã	'kind of fish'
36j. /ɔ̃ã/				
—	hɔ̃ãn	'equal'	hɔ̃ã	'cucumber'
	mɔ̃ãn	'famous'	mɔ̃ã	'great'
36k. /ẽã/				
—	bẽãn	'morning'	bẽã	'bent'
	sẽãn	'bath'	ʈẽã	'money'
	kẽãni	'groaning'	hẽã	'pretend to be ill'
36l. /ĩɔ̃/				
—	sĩɔ̃l	'shackle'	mĩɔ̃	'mix up, Imp.'
	sĩɔ̃n	'lean and thin'	zĩɔ̃	'to put fish in water'
	hĩɔ̃n	'peon'		
	hĩɔ̃r	'root'		
	zĩɔ̃l	'live'		
36m. /õɔ̃/	hõɔ̃n	'act of smelling'	hõɔ	smell, Caus. Prs'
	dõɔ̃n	'act of milking'		

3.6.3 Oral Diphthongs in SCB

Compared to NKB, SCB has seventeen diphthongs i.e. one more than the non-standard variety. The seventeenth diphthong in SCB is /iu/ unattested in NKB. The two dialects also vary in their variant selections of some other diphthongs. To be specific, /iɔ, ɛə, aɔ, oɔ, uɔ/ are unattested in SCB and in their stead SCB opts for /ɛo, eo, ao, ɔe, ɔo/. The two varieties agree in respect of the remaining eleven vowels i.e. /ui, ei, ai, oi, au, eu, ia, ua, oa, ɔa, ea/. The empirical support in favour of such a claim is provided by (37).

37a. /ui/

ui	'termite'	nuite	'to bend'	tui	pron.2 Sg, Non-Hon'
				d^hui	'wash, 1 Prs. Ind.'

37b. /ei/

ei	'this'	beiman	'ungrateful'	ʃei	'that'

37c. /ai/

ain	'law'	pain	'kind of tree'	cai	'want, 1 Prs. Ind.'
aibuɽo	'unmarried'	paik	'footman'	k^hai	'eat, 1 Prs. Ind.'

37d. /oi/

oi	'that'	boi	'book'	boiɽ^{h}a	'oar'

37e. /au/

auʃ	'autumnal rice'	baul	'saint'	lau	'gourd'

37f. /eu/

—-		neul	'mongoose'	keu	'someone'

37g. /ia/

—-		pial	'kind of tree'	dia	'lamp'

37h. /ua/

—-		duar	'door'		—-

37i. /oa/

oaɽ	'pillow cover'	poal	'hey'	k^hoa	'lose'

37j. /ɔa/

—		bɔano	'carrying, Caus.'	bɔa	'to carry'

37k. /ea/

—		peala	'cup'	nea	'take'

37l. /ɛo/

ɛoj	'to exchange'	kɛora	'kind of scent'	mɛo	'mew of cats'

37m. /eo/

—		deodar	'Deodar tree'	—	
		deog^{h}ɔr	'name of a place'	neoʈa	'doting'

37n. /ao/

aoʈano	'repeat'	paona	'due'	dao	'give, Imp.'
aota	'jurisdiction'	haolat	'lend money'	nao	'take, Imp.'

37o. /ɔe/

—		gɔena	'ornaments'	bɔe	'blows air etc.'
		mɔela	'dirt'	hɔe	'becomes'

37p. /ɔo/

—		ʃɔodgɔr	'merchant'	hɔo	'become Imp./Ind.'

37q. /iu/

—		ʃiuli	'kind of flower'	piu	'proper name'

3.6.4 Nasal Diphthongs in SCB

There exists a significant variance between the SCB oral and nasal diphthongs. First, the nasal diphthongs in SCB number sixteen in total as against seventeen oral diphthongs in the non-standard dialect: vowel /iu/ does not have any nasals counterpart with phonemic status.

Similarly, /ua, ɔa/ also do not allow nasal forms. Instead of these two, there is a separate nasal /õũ/. Finally, [ãõ] and [ĩũ] are only surface or phonetic versions having acquired nasality contextually.

38a. /ũĩ/

—-	—-	pũĩ	'a creeper'
		jũĩ	'jasmine'

38b. /ẽĩ/

—-	—-	hẽĩ	'a call of exertion.

38c./ãĩ/

—-	gãĩn	'singer'	cãĩ	'leader'

38d. /õĩ/

—-	põĩc^{h}a	'kind of bangle'
	bõĩci	'kind of fruit'

38e. /ãũ/

—-	pãũruṭi	'bread'	hãũ mãũ	'hue and cry'

38f. /ẽũ/

—-	—-	kẽũ kẽũ	'yelping of a dog'

38g. /ĩã/

—-	pĩãj	'onion'	mĩã	'Muslim gentleman'

38h. /õã/

—	—-	d^{h}õã	'smoke'

38i. /ẽã/

	pẽãj	'onion'	nea	'act of taking'
			mẽãd	'stipulated time'

38j. /ɛ̃õ/

—-	—-	gɛ̃õ	'rural'

38k. /ẽõ/				
—-		ʃẽõti	'kind of rose'	
		ɖẽõ	'kind of large ant'	
38l. /ãõ/				
—-	—-	nãõ	'boat'	
		bãõ	'unit of measuring the depth of water	
38m. /ɔ̃ẽ/				
—-	—-	pɔ̃ẽtriʃ	'thirty five'	
38n. [ɔ̃õ]				
—-	—-	nɔ̃õ	'you are not'	
38o. [ĩũ]				
—-	—-	mĩũ	'cry of a cat'	
38p. /õũ/				
—-		põũc^{h}ano	'to arrive'	—-
		kõũʃuli	'barrister'	

3.7 A Comparative Summary of the Vowels in SCB and NKB

In conclusion, I present a comparative picture of the vowel inventories of the two dialects of Bangla under study. As for the monophthongs the two dialects differ in that SCB has a seven vowel system consisted of /i e æ a ɔ o u/ while NKB has a six vowel system /i æ a ɔ o u/. Both the systems allow nasal counterparts for each of their respective oral vowels. As for the diphthongs, SCB has a maximum of seventeen oral diphthongs whereas NKB has one short i.e. sixteen. Of these first eleven vowels /ui, ei, ai, oi, au, eu, ia, ua, oa, ɔa, ea/ are shared by the two systems. They differ in the rest – compare vowels in bold font in the two columns E and F in (39) below. When it comes to the nasal diphthongs, the two dialects again differ in selecting the total number of such vowels: SCB has sixteen nasal diphthongs while NKB has thirteen. They however share nine diphthongs /ũĩ, ẽĩ, ãĩ, õĩ, ãũ, ẽũ, ĩã, õã, ẽã/. Of the rest, SCB selects /ɛ̃õ, ẽõ, ɔ̃ẽ, ɔ̃õ, õũ, ãõ/ phonemically and [ĩũ] allophonetically. In NKB the remaining nasal diphthongs are /ũã ɔ̃ã ĩɔ̃ õɔ̃/ which all enjoy independent phonemic status: For illustration one may refer to the columns G and H in (39) where all the differences between the oral and nasal vowels within each dialects are shown in bold fonts. The square braces indicate the non-phonemic status of the vowel concerned.

39.

Monophthongs				Diphthongs			
Oral		Nasal/Nasalized		Oral		Nasal/Nasalized	
A	B	C	D	E	F	G	H
SCB	NKB	SCB	NKB	SCB	NKB	SCB	NKB
1. i	1. i	1. ĩ	1. ĩ	1. ui	1. ui	1. ũĩ	1. ũĩ
2. e	2. æ	2. ẽ	2. æ̃	2. ei	2. ei	2. ẽĩ	2. ẽĩ
3. æ	3. a	3. æ̃	3. ã	3. ai	3. ai	3. ãĩ	3. ãĩ
4. a	4. ɔ	4. ã	4. ɔ̃	4. oi	4. oi	4. õĩ	4. õĩ
5. ɔ	5. o	5. ɔ̃	5. õ	5. au	5. au	5. ãũ	5. ãũ
6. o	6. u	6. õ	6. ũ	6. eu	6. eu	6. ẽũ	6. ẽũ
7. u		7. ũ		7. ia	7. ia	7. ĩã	7. ĩã
				8. ua	8. ua	8. õã	8. ũã
				9. oa	9. oa	9. ẽã	9. õa
				10. ɔa	10. ɔa	10. ɛ̃õ	10. ɔ̃ã
				11. ea	11. ea	11. ẽõ	11. ẽa
				12. ɛo	12. iɔ	12. ãõ	12. ĩɔ̃
				13. eo	13. ɛə	13. ɔ̃ẽ	13. õɔ̃
				14. ao	14. aɔ	14. [ɔ̃õ]	
				15. ɔe	15. oɔ	15. [ĩũ]	
				16. ɔo	16. uɔ	16. õũ	
				17. iu			

4.0 Conclusions

Variable phonology is a canonical feature of dialectal distinctions. In Bangla segmental phonology, the two dialects — the standard one i.e. SCB and a non-standard one namely NKB — examined in the present study, show significant differences. In respect of consonants it is found that:

a) the entire set of SCB voiced aspirated stops /bʰ, dʰ, ɖʰ, gʰ/ is lost in NKB;

b) /pʰ/ cannot be treated as part of the underlying inventory of the language, because although /pʰ/ exists in principle it is never phonetically realized: it is neutralized to [h] word initially and to [p] elsewhere.

c) /p pʰ/ and optionally /ʃ/ weaken to [h];

d) the SCB [h] is lost in NKB and the one found in NKB is only a derived segment with no existence in the underlying inventory;

d) the SCB affricates /c cʰ/ and /j jʰ/ get fricativized and fronted to /s/ and /z/ respectively;

e) the SCB retroflex flap /ɽ/ is phonetically simplified to r in NKB;

f) none of the dialects can be said to have clear cut evidence of semivowels;

The neat result of all these is that the NKB consonantal inventory stands drastically reduced to nineteen: with eight non-aspirated stops /p b t d ʈ ɖ k g/, three voiceless aspirated stops /tʰ ʈʰ kʰ/, three fricatives /s z ʃ/, three nasals /m n ŋ/, and one flap /r/ and one lateral /l/. SCB by contrast has twenty eight consonants consisting of sixteen plosives equally divided between aspirated and unaspirated ones /p b t d ʈ ɖ k g pʰ bʰ tʰ dʰ ʈʰ ɖʰ kʰ gʰ/, four affricates /c j cʰ jʰ/, two fricatives /ʃ h/ , three nasals /m n ŋ/, two flaps /r ɽ/ and one lateral /l/.

In case of vowels it has been noted that while SCB is a seven-vowel system with /i e æ a ɔ o u/, NKB is a six-vowel one containing

/i æ a ɔ o u/. Additionally, both the systems utilize nasality for phonemic contrast. In respect of complex vowels both use diphthongs both oral and nasal. Once again the two dialects differ notably: while SCB has seventeen oral diphthongs with phonemic status namely /ui, ei, ai, oi, au, eu, ia, ua, oa, ɔa, ea, ɛo, eo, ao, ɔe, ɔo, iu/, NKB has sixteen /ui, ei, ai, oi, au, eu, ia, ua, oa, ɔa, ea, iɔ, ɛə, aɔ, oɔ, uɔ/. As for nasal diphthongs SCB has sixteen /ũĩ, ẽĩ, ãĩ, õĩ, ãũ, ẽũ, ĩã, õã, ẽã, ɛ̃õ, ẽõ, ãõ, ɔ̃ẽ, õũ/, [ɔ̃õ], [ĩũ] of which nasality in the last two are contextually conditioned i.e. they acquire nasality from the preceding nasal consonant. In NKB, on the other hand, there are thirteen nasal diphthongs /ũĩ, ẽĩ, ãĩ, õĩ, ãũ, ẽũ, ĩã, õã, ẽã, ũã, ɔ̃ã, ĩɔ̃, õɔ̃/ all enjoying phonemic status.

A remarkable development to the direction of language change is the emergence of a High tone to compensate for the loss of the feature aspiration or [spr.gl] from the feature matrix for consonants. Beside this, there are found ample examples of vowel length being used contrastively in NKB, and such lengthening becomes operational both in consonance with and without tone, resulting in a sizable number of free variants. Given this rather confusing picture it requires further investigation to ascertain whether vowel lengthening is only a phonetic i.e. a surface phenomenon or it is gradually percolating deep down into the core phonology of featural distinctions of NKB. One of the offshoots of this drastically reduced number of consonants and, conversely, a large number of vowels (six oral monophthongs, six nasal monophthongs, sixteen oral diphthongs, and thirteen nasal diphthongs) along with distinctive vowel length and a High tone making up for the loss of aspiration, is that NKB appears to be a system distinctly vowel-dominated. The phenomenon of consonant weakening and deletion (discussed in Das 1996) so common in this dialect, produces innumerable cases of vowel coalescence resulting in sequences of three and four vowels. The cumulative effect of all these is that the dialect sounds a rather exotic one to the non-NKB speakers, endangering intelligibility and communication. In addition, the role of prosody (i.e. syllable template, foot pattern, nature of stress assignment — iterative or non-iterative, bounded or un-bounded etc.)

when examined in detail, may throw further light on this overall reductionist tendency of the NKB speakers. Such a study acquires special significance in the light of the upcoming theories like perceptual salience where consonants have an edge over vowels in respect of conveying morphological and other information (cf. Cote 1997, 2000a, 2000b, 2001, 2004, Hume 1999, Fleming 1995, Steriade 1999 etc.).

NOTES

1. It is customary in the literature of Bangla phonetics and phonology not to use the standard IPA symbols for the Bangla affricates. The reason behind this could be that the Bangla phoneticians perceive some differences between the affricates in Bangla and English. For more details one may refer to Bhattacharya (1988/1999).
2. In synchronic SCB these Sanskrit originated words are dying out of use. Still they can be found in very formal use.
3. In the final position deaspiration affects the obstruents even in SCB.
4. The change of $j^h \rightarrow j$ undergoes one more round of weakening resulting in /z/ in NKB. We shall have more discussion on fricativization of stops and affricates very shortly.
5. /k p/ are subject to optional deletion in between vowels in NKB and when not deleted /p/ survives as a bilabial fricative intervocalically. Since the matter is under further study, we shall for the present purpose continue to use the bilabial plosive instead of the bilabial fricative. Similarly [c] also becomes a fricative and realized as /s/. More discussion on fricativization follows.
6. This form of the word with $ṭ^h$ is only an intermediate form (indicated by the *), absent synchronically in NKB. The actual form of the obstruent survives as a voiced one i.e. ḍ in intervocalic positions.
7. Initial /p p^h/ obligatorily weaken to /h/ in NKB.
8. boza is alternatively also pronounced as hõza < ɸõza in NKB.
9. The phonetic implementation module or PIM may be equated with PF or Phonetic Form of Chomsky (1981a, 1986a. etc.).
10. The vowel [o] in NKB is phonetic i.e. it is the allophonic variety of the one notch lower back vowel /ɔ/. The occurrence of [o] is conditioned

by the presence of a [+high] vowel in the immediately succeeding syllable e.g. /nodi/ 'river' vs. /prɔman/ 'evidence'.

11. Intervocalic voicing of obstruents is a very productive process in NKB.

REFERENCES

Akmajian, A., R.A. Demers, A.K. Farmer, R.M. Harnish. 2001. *Linguistics: An Introduction to Language and Communication.* Cambridge (Mass.). MIT Press.

Bhattacharya, K.1988/1999. *Bengali Phonetic Reader.* Mysore, India, Central Institute of Indian Languages.

Chakraborty, R. 2006. Bangla (Bengali) vowels, Prepared for AKUSTYK for Praat.

//E:\AKUSTYK%20for%20Praat%20vowels%20of%languages.htm. Netaji Subhas Open University, Kolkata.

Chatterji, S.K. 1928. *A Bengali Phonetic Reader.* London, University of London Press.

Chomsky, N. 1981. *Lectures on Government and Binding*. Dordrecht, Foris.

_____ 1986. *Knowledge of Language: Its nature, origin and use*. New York, Praeger.

Chomsky, N. and M. Halle. 1968. *The Sound Pattern of English*. New York, Harper and Row.

Côté, M.H. 1997. Phonetic Salience and Consonant Cluster Simplification. In Benjamin Bruening et al (eds.) *PF: Papers at the Interface, MIT Working Papers in Linguistics* 29: 229-262. Cambridge (Mass.) MIT.

_____ 2000a. Consonant Cluster Phonotactics: A Perceptual Approach. Doctoral Dissertation. Cambridge (Mass.) MIT.

_____ 2000b. *The Perception of Stops in Post-consonantal Position and the Role of Auditory Cues in Stop Deletion.* Ms. Cambridge, Mass. MIT.

_____ 2001. *The Role of Perception in the Resolution of Consonant Clusters*. Presented at Conference on the Phonetics-phonology Interface, ZAS, Berlin.

_____ 2004. On Perception and Sonority in Cluster Simplification: Consonant Deletion in Icelandic Preterites. *Journal of Germanic Linguistics* 16.3: 203-204.

Das, S. 1996. Consonant Weakening in English and Bangla: A Lexical Phonological Investigation. M.Phil. Dissertation. Central Institute of English and Foreign Languages, Hyderabad.

Dasgupta, P. 2003. Bangla. In D. Jain and G. Cardona. (eds.) *The Indo-Aryan Languages*. London and New York, Routledge.

Flemming, E. 1995. Auditory Representations in Phonology. Doctoral Dissertation. University of California, Los Angeles.

_____ 2004. Contrast and Perceptual Distinctiveness. In B. Hayes et al (eds.), *Phonetically based Phonology*: 232-276. CUP

Goldsmith, J. 1990. *Autosegmental and Metrical Phonology*. Oxford, Blackwell.

Hai, M.A. 1993. *Dhvani Vijnan o Bangla Dhvani-Tattwa*. Dhaka, Mullick Brothers. (In Bangla)

Harris, J.W. 1969. *Spanish Phonology*. Cambridge (Mass.), MIT Press.

_____ 1985a. Autosegmental Phonology and Liquid Assimilation in Havana Spanish. In L. King and C. Maley (eds.) *Papers from the 13th Linguistic Symposium on Romance Language*. Amsterdam, Benjamins.

_____ J.W. 1985b. Spanish Diphthongization and Stress: A Paradox Resolved. *Phonology Year Book*. 2. 31-45.

Hume, E. and K. Johnson, (eds.) 2001. *The Role of Speech Perception in Phonology*. San Diego, Academic Press.

Kenstowicz, M. 2003. Salience and Similarity in Loanword Adaptation: A Case Study from Fijian. Cambridge, Mass. MIT. (ROA 219).

Paul, P.C. 1972. A Contrastive Study of the Sound Structure of English and Bengali. Doctoral Dissertation. IIT, Kharagpur, India.

Steriade, D. 1999. The Phonology of Perceptibility effects: the P-map and its Consequences for Constraint Organization. Ms. University of California, Los Angeles.

Vijaykrishnan, K.G. 1993. Dissimilation in Meitei. *SALA*. 15, 346-376.

2

Why does Tripura Bangla Sound so Different from Standard Bangla?[1]

1. Introduction

In a synchronic study instances of dialectal variation are canonical indications of language change in progress. In the absence of any scope for historico-derivational approach a comparative analysis of the related phenomena across dialects does and should provide vital insights into the general direction of change affecting the language as a whole. Born of such a presumption the present study seeks to make some futuristic statements about the would-be vowel inventory of Bangla language after having examined the vowel inventories of the Standard Colloquial Bangla (henceforth SCB) vis-à-vis Tripura Bangla (from now on TB, cf. Das 2001). Descriptively, a contrastive scenario prevails in the vowel inventories of the verbal-stems in SCB and TB: the former has done away with the high vowels i, u, while the latter strongly retains them; by contrast, while TB has nearly wiped out e and o, SCB tends to accord them almost the status of the unmarked. Considered from the universal perspective the SCB vowel inventory is at odds with cross-linguistic norms and if TB vowel is any indication to go by, the process of restoration to the universal dicta is perhaps on.

The other major focus of the present study is a more theoretical one aimed at providing a principled account to the remnants of the dying vocalic segments of TB. It is found that these segments namely e and o which are otherwise on the verge of extinction from the system are still retained only in positions which are canonically treated as prosodic heads such as the most prominent syllable in a prosodic word. In the literature this is known as positional faithfulness i.e. faithful retention of underlying features of segments in prosodically strong positions. In course of the present study, this phenomenon is alternatively referred to as prosodic licensing, resisted neutralization etc. I shall wind up the paper by providing some hints at the way the language is likely to evolve in the days to come.

The organization of the paper is as follows. Following the Introduction (Section 1), Section 2 presents the vowel inventories of SCB and TB with greater focus on the latter. Section 3 deals with the ɛ ~ e alternation in TB and its implications for the latter's vowel inventory. Section 4 carries out a similar exercise in respect of ɔ ~ o. Section 5 discusses the issue of positional faithfulness in the midst of a prevalent picture of restructuring affecting the vowel system of TB. Section 6 contains a brief discussion on the theoretical approach to positional faithfulness.

2. Vowel Inventories

2.1 SCB Vowels

Irrespective of their theoretical persuasion, the majority of the researchers (including Chattterji 1926, Sarkar 1979, 1983-84, Dasgupta 1982, Paul 1985, 1986, Dan 1992, Ghosh 1996 etc.) working on the various aspects of Bangla phonology has argued for a seven-vowel system in SCB. These are /i, e, ɛ, a, ɔ, o, u/. Going one step further in respect of subtlety of analysis and working on SCB vowel harmony with special reference to the verbal forms, Ghosh (1996) claims that Bangla verbal forms have two vowel systems: a five vowel for the verbal stems and a seven vowel system for the suffixes. The former includes /e, ɛ, a, ɔ, o/ (i.e. excluding the high vowels) and the latter /i, e, ɛ, a, ɔ, o, u/. It is surprising to note that the SCB verbal stems systematically lack the two high vowel /i, u/ while even the simplest of vowel systems – a three-vowel system containing /i, u, a/ — attested in natural languages make use of these peripheral points in the vowel space. We shall have more discussion on this accidental (?) gap in the utilization of the vowel space in Bangla before long.

With these observations for the standard dialect in mind, let us survey the distribution of vowels in TB. To start with we make a general inspection of the non-verbal stems and then come back to verbal stems and then come back to verbal roots before we arrive at a comprehensive picture of the underlying inventory of vowels in TB.

2.2 Distribution of vowels in nonverbal stems in TB

1. a. /i/ represents the front high unrounded vowel uniformly distributed over the initial, medial and final positions:

Initial	Medial	Final
iɖal 'stone throw'	hiʃab 'calculation'	aɖali 'lick'
indur 'rat'	gilu 'brain'	nodi 'river'

1b. /e/ is a front mid unrounded vowel which also is attested in all positions.

esi	'sneezing'	keɖi	'small'	ke	'who'
eʈki	'hiccup'	geɖi	'neck'	te	'he'

1c. [2]/ɛ/ is a front low unrounded vowel and its occurrence is disallowed finally.

ɛk	'one'	pɛk	'clay'	—
ɛtɔ	'so much'	pɛrɔt	'untidy person'	

1d. /a/ is a back centralized low vowel, found in all positions.

aga	'top/peak'	salu	'smart'	oza	'exorcist'
aɖu	'knee'	pɔtaka	'flag'	pola	'boy'

1e. /ɔ/ is a back low rounded vowel, which is found in all places of occurrences.

ɔlɔʃ	'idle'	rɔg	'artery/vein'	ɔlpɔ	'little bit'
ɔga	'stupid'	bɔlɔd	'bullock'	duʃʈɔ	'naughty'

1f. /o/ is a back mid rounded vowel and it occurs in all positions.

oʃud	'medicine'	zora	'joint'	'bo'	'bride'
ogɔl	'kind of fish'	gora	'horse'	—	

1g. /u/ is the back high rounded vowel occurring in all the three places.

ural	'flight'	p^hul	'flower'	abu	'baby'
una	'less by one'	dul	'earring'	alu	'potato'

3. ɛ~e alternation and implications for vowel inventory

It appears from the above data that there are seven vowels /i, e, ɛ, a, ɔ, o, u/ in TB. But before we arrive at any conclusive decision a close scrutiny of the distributional gap noted in case of ɛ (cf. 1c.) is necessary. It would be unrewarding, however, to consider this phenomenon in isolation. A careful observation reveals that there exists a kind of complementarity between e and e: e occurs in all the positions while e does only non-finally. This along with the phonetic proximity that the two share might give one the impression that ɛ is in fact a positional variant of e. But this could be easily argued against. Word initial and word medial occurrence of e is exclusively conditioned by the presence of a following high vowel.

2.	eli	'whining'	zeɖu	'father's elder brother'
	beʃi	'much'	lezur	'tail'
	beɖi	'woman'	kelu	'SCB, slang'

Besides, there are very few words with final e in TB. ke 'who', te 'he, familiar' ze 'who', he 's/he', de 'give/surname', ne 'take' perhaps exhaust the list of monomorphemic words with final e.[3] This means, word finally, use of neither e nor ɛ is productive in monomorphemic sequences; but non-finally the latter enjoys a greater distributional freedom as we see below.

3.	ɛk	'one'	ɛmɔn	'like this'	kɛra	'centipede'
	ɛkla	'alone'	kɛmne	'how'	bɛla	'time'

ɛlai	'profuse'	tɛrɔ	'thirteen'	lɛz	'tail'
ɛlaka	'area'	bɛtɔn	'salary'	dɛʃ	'country'

Unlike e, ɛ can occur in a closed syllable and also before any non-high vowel. On the basis of the above one could feel justified to say that e is a variant of ɛ.

Given these conflicting possibilities of either of the vowels being the basic, one would do better to look for minimal pairs involving the two as clinching evidence for the phonemic status of both. Though very rare there is still proof that the two vowels are in fact distinctive in TB. They contrast medially in dɛk 'see, Present imperative (order)': dek 'give, Future imperative, 3P)'; nek 'take, Future imperative 3P': nɛk 'tendency'. The proof of the fact that the vowel in dɛk & nɛk and the one dek and nek are not the same is also available from their different realization under the suffixation of the same morpheme whose high vowel provides the trigger for alternation in the root vowel.

4.	Verb root	Suffix		
	dɛk	i	→ dehi	'see. 1P, Pres.'[4]
	de	i	→ dii	'give, 1P, Pres.'
	ne	i	→ nii	'take, IP, Pres.'

Both the vowels e and ɛ undergo harmonic raising by one notch in the vertical scale of vowel space under the influence of the following suffixal high vowel. But while the former reaches to e, the front mid high vowel, the other touches the front high mark symbolized by i. This is therefore a strong piece of evidence that ɛ and e are two distinct vowels in TB.

However, it is difficult to build up a strong case in favour of e belonging to the core inventory of TB. In fact the above structuralist diagnostic gives only a static and imperfect view of the underlying inventory of a language and fails to say anything about a language in change. This is because there are not many non-derived lexical items including verbal stems in this dialect, which contain e without being followed by a high vowel. A survey of the verb roots reveals that there are only two roots de and ne in TB, which retain e against an overwhelming trend of restructuring the verbal roots by substituting i for e. This is proved by the following comparison of the same verbal roots in SCB and TB.[5]

5.

SCB	TB		SCB	TB	
ʃekʰ	ʃik	'learn'	gel	gil	'swallow'
ken	kin	'buy'	ʈep	ʈip	'press'
peʈ	piʈ	'beat'	cen	sin	'recognize'
pʰer	pʰir	'return'	gʰer	gir	'surround'
cʰeɽ	sir	'tear'	ʈek	ʈik	'last'

All the verbal roots containing e in SCB are realized with i in TB. de and ne (not in (5)) stand out as exceptions as these roots are pronounced identically in both the dialects. It is logical therefore to say that de and ne are just two remnants reflecting the transitional phase of the vowel system of TB neutralizing the contrast between e and i in favour of the later.

Beside verbal roots underived lexical items belonging to various other categories also show this general tendency of restructuring. Compare for instance the following set of words belonging to SCB and TB.

6.

SCB	TB		SCB	TB	
pẽaj	piaz	'onion'	beɽal	biral/bilai	'cat'
bʰeja	biza	'wet'	ʃekoɽ	ʃikɔr	'root'
teto	tita	'bitter'	ʃeal	ʃial	'fox'
jed	zid	'anger'	ʃeddo	ʃiddɔ	'boiled'
petol	pitɔl	'brass'	bʰetor	bitɔr	'inside'

Against this general backdrop of e neutralizing to i, a logical question crops up regarding the underlying identity of e present in so many mono-morphemic sequences in TB. In the absence of alternation it becomes difficult to establish the underlying form of any linguistic item. A null hypothetic suggestion would be to hold the underlying representation as identical to the surface realization. By such an account e will be accorded a substantial position in the core inventory of segments of TB and this certainly is contradicted by the preceding observations (cf. 5-6) where e is found to be neutralizing to i in TB. This change is independent of any phonological conditioning. In fact any instance of harmonic alternation of e~i induced by a trigger, palpable or otherwise, other than those in the members of the verbal paradigms of de and ne is unattested in TB.[6] Given this overall absence of any harmonic e~i alternation on the one hand and the general picture of e~i neutralization on the other, one has a strong reservation against the underlying presence of e in TB stems. We have therefore no concrete suggestion as yet for what could be the underlying form of the surface e in TB.

Contrary to the absence of e~i alternation, there is a large number of cases where ɛ harmonizes to e under the influence of a suffixal high vowel.[7] The following set of examples representing various lexical categories in both derivational and inflectional morphology, bear this out.

7a. Verbal inflection

Root	Suffix		
lɛk	i	→ leχi/ lehi	'write, 1P. Press'
dɛk	i	→ deχi/ dehi	'see, 1P. Pres.'
bɛs	i	→besi	'sell, 1P. Pres.'

7b. Denominal adjectives/nouns

Noun		Suffix		
dɛʃ	'country'	i	→deʃi	'native'
tɛz	'anger'	i	→tezi	'angry'
kɛʃ	'hair'	i	→keʃi	'hairy' [8]
beʃ	'dress'	i	→beʃi	'person wearing that dress/look'

7c. Nominal inflections: gender

Noun		Suffix		
bɛɖa	'male'	i	→beɖi	'female'
zɛɖa	'uncle'	i	→zeɖi	'aunt'
bɛra	'ram'	i	→beri	'ewe'

In all the examples above the surface realization of e is contingent upon the presence of the suffixal high vowel in the following syllable and more significantly, in all cases the stem contains ɛ. This ɛ~e alternation is therefore a strong piece of evidence that a rule of harmonic raising involving the two vowels is already there.

For further corroboration of the same phenomenon, let us now introduce evidence from mono-morphemic sequences. In such sequences, in the absence of any palpable harmonic alternation, distributional properties of a particular segment functions as a canonical diagnostic. On the strength of the insight achieved from the derivational phenomena in (7), it may be hypothesized that e occurs only in a context preceding a high vowel. Examples in (2.2) above have already familiarized us with this phenomenon. However, a thorough survey is well warranted for a clear-cut statement. Let us look at the following examples, which are uniformly non-derived.

8a.	Word		b.	Word	
	σ	σ		σ	σ
	e	i/u		*e	e/o

9a.			b.		
	peti	'petty'		belun	'balloon'
	peʃi	'muscle'		reɖu	'radio'
	beli	'kind of flower'		ketu	'ninth planet'
	keɖi	'small'		renu	'pollen'
	meni	'kind of fish'		meru	'polar'
	tribeni	'confluence of three rivers'		ʃumeru	'North Pole'

No underived word in TB instantiates the distribution of e graphically presented in (8b). In fact the closest approximation to a sequence of 'e e' across syllable is 'ɛ ɛ': ɖɛrɛʃ 'lady's finger', bɛrɛʃ 'bull'. Similarly a phonotactic restriction against occurrence of e and o in successive syllables results in the realization of SCB words like the following with a sequence of ɛ and ɔ in TB.

10.

SCB	TB		SCB	TB	
tero	tɛrɔ	'thirteen'	reʃon	rɛʃɔn	'provisions'
beton	bɛtɔn	'salary'	beʃon	bɛʃɔn	'powdered pulse'
reʃom	rɛʃɔm	'silk'			

Consideration of the words in (9-10) shows that the deciding factor behind the occurrence of e is the presence of the succeeding high vowel even in mono-morphemes. So let us now put together the facts about the front vowels in TB and their possible implications for the vowel inventory.

11. (a) e never harmonizes to i (except in de and ne)
    (b) e neutralizes to i
    (c) ɛ harmonizes to e under influence of the following high vowel
    (d) Presence of e in monomorphemes is preconditioned by the presence of a succeeding high vowel.
    (e) A non-high vowel in the following syllable exercises a lowering effect on the preceding e in TB vis-à-vis SCB.

By analyzing the above facts it can be logically deduced that there is a virtual gap in the utilization of the vowel space in TB compared to that in SCB. The stem phonology of TB has hardly any underlying e and this gap is filled up at the phonetic level by harmonic raising of the next lower vowel i.e., ɛ to e. This dispersion of the vowel quality towards the periphery runs counter to the observed phenomenon in SCB, especially in the verbal stems which instantiate a systematic absence of high vowel i (and also u) and the gap is filled up by harmonic raising of the next lower vowel e. A comparative picture of the situations prevailing in the two varieties of Bangla can be diagrammatically presented as in (12).

12a.	SCB	b. TB
	*i	i
	↑	
	e	*e
		↑
	ɛ	ɛ

* indicates the absence of the concerned vowel in the underlying inventory.

By the standard of universal conventions this is a rather strange situation. For universally because of their perceptual salience peripheral vowels are treated as 'unmarked' and hence 'primary'. Consequently, as Crothers (1978), notes even the smallest of the known systems tends to contain (only) high and low vowels, and the complexity of quality distinction increases along the vertical axes in proportion to the number of points contrastively exploited by a particular language in between the peripheries. SCB stands out as an odd exception in this respect. The process of major restructuring supplanting e with i observed in TB is therefore a logical development towards restoring the Bangla vowel system in general to the dicta of universal conventions. May be in course of time this restoration process will also invade through the lexicon of the standard variety if the existing rule of harmonic alternation of e~i in SCB is any indication to go by. Seen in this light the disturbing remnants of underlying e in TB should be construed as symptomatic of transitional instability.

4. ɔ~o Alternation and Implication for Vowel Inventory

A similar picture emerges in respect of the underlying relation between o and ɔ in TB. Compared to the latter, independent occurrences of the former in non-initial position is highly restricted. bo 'bride' (1f) is perhaps the only underived word with final o.[9] In the non-final position occurrence of o is preconditioned by the presence of a succeeding high vowel unless o occurs in the *initial* syllable:[10] nɔd 'river' ~ nodi 'river', gɔd 'routine' ~ godi 'cushion', gɔr 'home' ~ gori 'watch' etc. Again distributionally ɔ enjoys a much greater freedom than o. Understandably such factors point towards a so-called complementary relationship between the two. But such an option is at once preempted by the presence of such contrastive occurrence of the two vowels in pairs of words like the following.

13. rɔg	'artery/vein'	tɔla	'bottom'	gɔla	'throat'
rog	'disease'	tola	'unit of weight'	gola	'granary'

We have encountered a similar paradox in the previous section in respect of ascertaining the underlying identity of e and ɛ; and in the ultimate analysis this conflicting state of affairs is found to be indicative of a deep rooted process of restructuring underway in the vowel inventory of TB. Perhaps we are in for another such experience especially given the fact that o is also a non-peripheral vowel like e and across languages, preference for non-peripheral vowel is more marked than that for peripheral ones. A thorough inquiry of the phenomenon is therefore in order.

Since the present study is specific to stem vowels and since verbal stems constitute a sizable body of it, let us start with a comparative survey of the verb roots of SCB and TB to see if there is any instance of root vowels gravitating towards u from o. Remember, corresponding evidence in respect of e~i provided the first major argument in favour of the absence of e in the underlying inventory of TB. Let us therefore consider the following set of data.

14a.			b.		
SCB	TB		SCB	TB	
k^hõɽ	k^hor	'dig'	boj	buz	'understand'
c^hol	sol	'peel off'	g^hor	gur	'turn around'
jor	zor	'attach'	oʈ^h	uʈ	'get up'
tol	tol	'lift'	k^hõʈ	k^huʈ	'erase with nail'
k^hol	k^hol	'open'	gol	gul	'dilute'

doʃ	doʃ	'blame'	ʃon	ʃun	'hear'
ʃo	ʃo	'sleep'	j^hol	zul	'swing'
t^ho	t^ho	'keep'	c^hoʈ	suʈ	'run'
d^ho	do	'wash'	b^hol	bul	'forget'
ro	ro	'plant'	ʃod	ʃud	'repay'
no	no	'bend forward'	bon	bun	'weave'
c^hõ	so	'touch'	poʃ	puʃ	'rear'
do	do	'milk'	j^hõk	zuk	'bend'

In all the words above the verbal form for the Second Person Imperative (ordinary) is treated as the root because of the absence of any overt morphological augment. (14) contains a fairly exhaustive survey of verbal roots containing both o and u. In (14a) the controversial root vowel is identical both in the standard and the non-standard dialects. But an equal number of roots also instantiates restructuring of o to u as shown in (14b).[11] Though the picture is not as radical as that prevailing in case of e~i noted in (5), nevertheless there is no denying the fact that the process of supplanting o with u has already diffused through a sizable chunk of the TB lexicon. Again, that this process of o ~ u neutralization is not confined to verb roots alone is proved by the following set of cross-categorial non-derived words from TB.

15.

SCB	TB		SCB	TB	
j^hol	zol~zul	'gravy'	kol	kol~kul	'lap'
lol	lol~lul	'saliva'	rog	rog~rug	'disease'
kona	kona~kuna	'corner'	loha	loa~lua	'iron'
gõʃai	gõʃai~guʃai	'preceptor'	kumɽo	komra~kumra	'pumpkin'

We have already noticed that for harmonic alternation physical presence of the trigger is commonplace in TB both in morphologically simple and complex circumstances.[12] Consequently, absence of any succeeding high vowel functioning as a trigger rules out the possibility of harmonic raising as opposed to neutralization. Optionality in this respect merely signifies a state of transitional indeterminacy.

(14) and (15) put together argue for the fact that there exists a strong undercurrent of replacing o with u in TB though the degree of success in this respect is not as spectacular as in case of e~i. Nearly 50% of verb roots (cf. 14b) have undergone vowel neutralization in favour of the peripheral vowel u[13] and the picture is symmetrical to that of e~i neutralization. But what is perhaps more important from the theoretical point of view is that it seeks to fill up the underlying gap in the vowel inventory of Bangla which (qua Ghosh 1996) lacks the high vowels i and u against the universal practice of giving primacy to peripheral vowels over medial ones. Understandably such a proposition entails the responsibility of critically responding to the host of counter examples offered by TB.

For a clearer view of the underlying identity of these counter examples it is advisable to start out with the palpable cases of alternations for which derived context are the ideal. As in case of other alternations discussed in the preceding section the harmony factor rests in the suffixal high vowel. Counter examples to o~u neutralization fall into two categories: those verbal roots which are presumably yet to undergo restructuring; and those, which come to contain o as a consequence of raising under suffixation. We shall address the former in a subsequent section for reasons to be clear in due course. In the latter case the root vowel obviously originates as ɔ i.e., one notch down in the vertical scale as we notice in the following.

16. Verb roots	Suffix			
sɔl	i	→	soli	'walk, 1P. Press.'
ʃɔr	i	→	ʃori	'move aside, 1P, Press.'

gɔn	i	→	goni	'count, 1P, Press.'
lɔr	i	→	lori	'waver, 1P, Press.'

The conclusion is the same as that for ɛ~e alternation: ɔ is raised to fill up the virtual vacuum created by the neutralization of o to u. But this raising is only a surface phenomenon and fails to affect the underlying inventory: ɔ nowhere neutralizes to o.

Since the scope of present inquiry is primarily confined within stems, for clinching evidence one should look at the non-alternating sequences and in this respect examining the phonotactics of vowel distribution provides the chief methodological help. Guided by the insight offered by the derived contexts in (16) we expect to find o in a word provided it is followed by a high vowel in the next syllable.

17a.

18a.			b.		
	boli	'ritual'		kosu	'arum'
	kobi	'poet'		modu	'honey'
	kosi	'tender'		goru	'cow'
	nodi	'river'		zorul	'nevus'
	ʃorir	'body'		korul	'bamboo shoots'
	gorib	'poor'		korun	'sad'
	ɔtoʃi	'kind of flower'		roʃun	'garlic'

Illustrations in (18) justify the claim that for phonotactic reasons occurrence of o is dependent upon a following high vowel. This claim is indirectly supported by the following set of negative evidence derived through a comparison of some SCB words having a sequence of 'ɔ o' across syllable boundary with their counterparts in TB. In the latter the vowel of the second syllable weakens to ɔ since it is not licensed by a succeeding high vowel.

19.

SCB	TB		SCB	TB	
ʃɔrot	ʃɔrɔt	'autumn'	kɔlom	kɔlɔm	'pen'
gajor	gazɔr	'carrot'	ʃɔhor	ʃɔhɔr	'city'
naṭok	naṭɔk	'drama'	k^hɔbor	k^hɔbɔr	'news'
gɔrom	gɔrɔm	'hot'	bɔʃontɔ	bɔʃɔntɔ	'spring time'

No monomorphemic word in TB has a sequence of 'o e'. The SCB sequence of 'o o' is reduced to 'o ɔ' in the absence of a succeeding high vowels in words like ʃolo (SCB) → ʃolɔ (TB) 'sixteen', gopon (SCB) → gopɔn (TB) 'secret' etc. We do not address here the issue of what protects the initial o from being reduced to ɔ since a detailed discussion follows on this in the succeeding section.

Let us now summarize the phonological facts concerning o and what do they imply for the status of o in the underlying system of TB.

20. a) A major restructuring undergoing in TB lexicon enforces neutralization of o to u.

b) ɔ harmonizes to o under influence of the following high vowel.

c) Presence of o in monomorphemes is conditioned by the presence of a succeeding high vowel.

The gist of the whole story is that there is another gap in the vowel inventory of TB in the form of the absence of o. But this gap is yet to emerge as an absolute one compared to the near-complete one in case of e. This gap however is phonetically filled up for surface requirement by harmonic raising of the next low vowel ɔ. This restructuring of the vowel inventory is in perfect harmony with the cross-linguistic practice of according unmarked value to the peripheral vowels compared to the non-peripheral ones. Seen in this universal perspective, certain directions of language change becomes predictable from the analysis of the emergent vowel inventory: in the long run TB, and perhaps Bangla as a whole, may move towards a five vowel system for non-derived lexical items with the following members: i, u, ɛ, ɔ, a; presence of e and o will be restricted to surface alternation.

5. A Vowel System in Change and Evidence for Positional Faithfulness

In course of this brief exposition of the underlying inventory of vowels in TB and Bangla in general, we have seen that the undercurrent of restructuring which is gradually eroding the phonemic basis of e and o, has achieved only 50% success in case of o in comparison to the degree of its success registered in respect of e. In the latter instance the process is nearly complete.

It would be theoretically interesting to examine the distribution of the so-called exceptional occurrences of e and o in TB. In (21) we formalize the contexts of the occurrence of the latter.

21. a. # (C)o(C)
    b. #Co.CV (C)
    c. (. .).Co.Ci/u (C)

(21a-b) imply that o can occur in the initial syllable irrespective of the presence and nature of the following vowel. We have already seen the presence of i, u, ɔ, a in the syllable following the one containing o. That e can also occur following o is proved by the following examples from derived contexts: tol-e 'lift, 3P. Pres.', kʰol-e 'open, 3P. Press.' kol-e 'lap, Loc.' etc. In all other contexts i.e. in word medial syllables, occurrence of o is strictly determined by the presence of a high vowel in the following syllable (cf. 21c). Stated differently, word-internal distribution of o is phonotactically determined, as it is contingent upon a succeeding high vowel. Consequently there is some phonetic grounding in the word internal distribution of o in the form of what Ghosh (1996) following Pulleyblank (1993) designates as [+ATR] harmony while discussing similar cases in SCB. In fact evidence from derived contexts[14] (cf.16) show that stem internal ɔ harmonizes to o in response to [+ATR] harmony present in the suffixal high vowel. By contrast no such factor is perceptibly at work in enforcing the occurrence of o in word initial syllables. The question to ask therefore is what is so special about the initial syllable that can be a legitimate licensor of an otherwise marked segment. Answer to this question lies in the concept of prosodic licensing or faithfulness to prosodic heads.

The occurrence of o is restricted only to the word-initial syllable unless it is followed by high vowel in the next syllable. Obviously this word-initial syllable enjoys some special status compared to others in the word. In TB normally the initial syllable is stressed, and seen in the context of the phonotactics of o, this implies that this vowel can occur only in a stressed syllable. In that case we expect to find o in all foot initial syllables since TB constructs trochees from left to right (cf. Das 2001). But since o is not attested in the head syllable of other than the initial foot (when not licensed by a succeeding high vowel), the logical conclusion to be drawn is that occurrence of this marked segment is restricted to iteration initial foot which being the head foot universally contains the most prominently stressed syllable. In TB the locus of o is thus the most prominent syllable in an underived word.[15] Obviously this is a case of *prosodically conditioned licensing* or *faithfulness to prosodic head*; and this provides clinching evidence in favour of the assumption that TB makes distinction between primary and (at least) secondary stresses[16]. An even stronger evidence for o being licensed only in primary stressed syllable in TB is offered by the following set of trisyllables in which the heavy second syllable attracts primary stress and consequently ensures the preservation of the underlying featural identities of the vowel it contains. A comparison with the corresponding SCB forms makes the point clear.

22. SCB	TB	
ʃujó ggɔ	ʃuzóiggɔ	'perfectly eligible'
aróggɔ	aroíggɔ	'curable'
alóʃʃɔ	aloíʃʃɔ	'idleness'
acódna	asódna	'idiot, sl'
—	apóŋɖa	'wicked, sl'
agʰómʈa	agómɖa[17]	'woman without headgear'

Remnants of e found only in the initial syllable of six mono-morphemic (mono-syllabic) words — ke 'who, ze 'who rel.' te 'he', he '(s)he', de 'give' and ne 'take' – further substantiate the observation that TB makes distinction between primary and secondary stresses: this marked vowel is licensed only in the most prominent syllable of an underived word. The reason why e does not occur even in disyllables unless licensed by a succeeding high vowel is perhaps because its restructuring is nearly complete unlike that of o.

In sum, we have strong evidence from the vowel phonology of TB in support of there being a distinction between the primary and non-primary levels of prominence in Bangla language. The two marked vowels e and o, which are gradually losing their phonemic status as a consequence of restructuring of the vowel inventory of Bangla, can still survive independently –i.e. when not licensed by succeeding high vowel – iff they occur in the most prominent syllable of the word. A principled explanation of the phenomenon is possible if licensing is looked upon as faithfulness to prosodic heads popularly known in the literature as Prosodic Licensing.

6. Positional faithfulness (or Prosodic Licensing) and Optimality Theory

The concept of prosodic licensing as originally propounded in Ito (1988) is a general theory of prosodic licensing to account for syllable-based phonotactics. She interprets syllabification as template matching. Building on McCarthy's (1979) idea that phonemic material that fails to map to the template is suppressed, she extends stray erasure to a general constraint on phonological representation: all phonological segments must be prosodically licensed. There are two ways to achieve prosodic licensing: association to the syllabic template or declaration as extra-syllabic at the edge of the relevant prosodic domain (for marginal consonant clusters). Material that is not prosodically licensed is deleted by Stray Erasure.

Since Ito's primary concern was syllabification and syllable-based phonotactics, the specific details of her theory do not concern us directly here. But the very concept of prosodic licensing abstracted away from the details of its original proposal and its potential expandability to other prosodic categories has rendered it an attractive theoretical apparatus in the subsequent research in phonology (cf. Goldsmith 1990, Kaye, Lowenstamm, and Vergnaud 1990, Steriade 1995). To be se specific, just as there can be intra-syllabic phonotactic restrictions against the occurrence of a certain segment or segment sequence in a designated position such as onset or coda in a particular language, there can be phonotactic restrictions against the occurrence of a particular segment in a syllable if the latter does not occupy a designated position in the higher prosodic categories such as foot, prosodic word etc.

In OT the concept of prosodic licensing is a more generalized one in the sense that OT looks upon licensing as faithfulness to prosodic heads or as positional faithfulness. "There are", to quote Beckman (1998:vii) "a variety of phonological asymmetries exhibited by segments which appear in perceptually or psycho-linguistically prominent positions such as roots, root-initial syllables, stressed syllables, and syllable onsets. In such positions, segmental or featural contrasts are often maintained, though they may be neutralized in non-prominent positions. Segments in prominent positions frequently trigger phonological processes such as assimilation, dissimilation and vowel harmony; conversely, they often block or resist the application of these processes." Resistance to neutralization is attributed to constraints that license features in specific positions, which are linguistically privileged. The OT mechanism to capture prosodic licensing is a ranking schema in which markedness constraints are sandwiched between positional and general faithfulness constraints: IO-Faithfulness (*prominent position*) >> Markedness >> IO-Faithfulness (*general*). An OT analysis however has not been attempted here.

Notes

1. This paper was presented at the 25th All India Conference of Linguists of the Linguistic Society of India, Nov. 26-28, 2002, at CU, Kolkata, as "Positional Faithfulness and Resisted Neutralization in the vowel

inventory of Tripura Bangla". I am thankful to the audience for the comments which have helped in upgrading the paper.

2. ɛ in TB approximates very closely æ. But this finer distinction has been kept out of the purview of the present discussion as because the intention here is a comparative analysis between the vowel systems of TB and SCB.

3. Two other words frequently used are aste 'slowly' and baze 'useless'. The first one is a Persian loan in Bangla (<ahista) and as the gloss shows it behaves like a derived adverb. Chaterji (1926) does not enter baze (SCB baje) as a lexical item of Bangla in its present sense. Though of doubtful origin, its semantic affinity with the Sanskrit derived adjective bordʒyo 'to be rejected' may be argued for. The latter also has its regular survivor in SCB compounds like borjo podartho "waste'. Considered thus both aste and baze should be treated as derived words as the native speakers in fact do.

4. No word can be formed by suffixing -i to nɛk. However, a non-sense word like /neki/ is easily acceptable.

5. In all these cases verbal root corresponds to the Second Person Imperative (ordinary) form, which bears no overt morphological marker.

6. Ghosh (1996) explains harmonic raising of e to i (among others) in SCB as an instance of [+ATR] spreading from a phonetically present or deleted high vowel: ken → kini/kinlam, gel → gili/gilbe etc. In addition he also quotes Basu (1975) that SCB attests instances of Mutual Vowel Harmony whereby bilat → bilet → bilet-i → biliti 'foreign, deʃi → diʃi 'native' etc. Such alternations are unattested in TB.

7. Unlike in SCB verbal paradigm for these roots, presence of the suffixal high vowel in the inflective is a must in TB: bɛs-i → besi, but bɛs-il-am → bɛslam/ *beslam etc. This distinction in terms of transparency of the conditioning factor is likely to have a substantial bearing on the interpretation of vowel harmony in TB as opposed to that in SCB. Discussion of vowel harmony in TB is however outside the purview of this paper.

8. This and the words like the following normally exist as the second member of compounds which function both as noun and adjective:

kalo-kɛʃ → kalokeʃi 'black haired (fem. Noun or Adjective), sɔddɔ-bɛʃ → sɔddɔbeʃi 'disguised (Noun or Adjective).

9. go, lo are both clitics as they can occur only as an adage to another word: hɛ̃)-go, ma-go, koi-lo, ʃoi-lo etc. Words like balo 'well', kalo 'black' are latest entries and bear strong signs of SCB. The typical TB words for these are bala and kala. ko 'where' is again, a contracted form of more commonly used koi. In the non-final position occurrence of o is preconditioned by the presence of a succeeding high vowel unless o occurs in the initial syllable.

10. The word 'initial' is deliberately italicized to imply that the statement is only partially true since, as argued convincingly in Das (2001), o can occur independently (i.e. without being licensed by a high vowel in the following syllable) only if the host syllable is the most prominent one in the word.

11. Significantly, at least one verb root meaning 'to count' undergoes restructuring through vowel lowering in TB vis-à-vis SCB: gon (SCB) → gɔn (TB). This is exactly like what happens in case of the verb meaning 'to write' where SCB e is lowered to ɛ in the TB counterpart: lek^h (SCB) → lɛk (TB).

12. There are at least two counter examples where the trigger is physically absent in the context: tol → tultam 'lift, 1P. Habitual Past', k^hol → k^hultam 'open, 1P. Habitual Past'.

13. The remaining 50% of the verb root containing o undergo harmonic raising under the influence of suffixal high vowel as it happens also in SCB. Such phonologically conditioned alternations being theoretically inconsequential for the underlying inventory, do not merit focused consideration here.

14. In derived words it is primarily the presence of the suffixal high vowel that ensures the occurrence of o in the immediately preceding syllable which inevitably belongs to the stem whether initial or not: ʃahɔʃ-i ʃahoʃi 'courageous', manɔb-i → manobi 'woman', kɔr-i → kori 'do. 1P. Press.' However if the monosyllabic stem contains o and that syllable occupies the initial position in the derived word the role of the suffuxal vowel is irrelevant: tol-ɔn → tolɔn 'lifting', zor-ɔn →zorɔn 'attaching' etc.

15. The following set of words is likely to prove a potential source of counterexamples especially due to progressive increase in literacy rate as well as the influence of SCB. But a careful observation shows that the native TB speakers are more prone to replace o in the SCB counterparts of the words with u and less often with ɔ. alocɔna (SCB)~ alusɔna (TB) 'discussion', ʃujog (SCB)~ʃuzug (TB) 'chance', ʃoja (SCB)~ʃuja (TB) 'straight', niyog (SCB)~niyug (TB) 'appointment', ʃɔŋjojon (SCB) ~ ʃɔŋzuzon (TB) 'addition' etc.

16. Attempt to make further distinction in the degrees of prominence is theoretically unrewarding and hence not pursued here.

17. An objection may be raised against the point being made here on the basis of the counterexamples like anɔ'ndɔ 'joy', ɔhɔ'ŋkar 'pride', aʃɔ'ŋka 'apprehension' etc. But such an objection is at once nullified if it is remembered that all that we are advocating for is that neutralization of o to ɔ or u is a part of the general restructuring (on going) of the vowel inventory of TB. The remnants of o are attested only in the most prominent syllable of a word thanks to the well-attested phenomenon of faithfulness to prosodic heads.

References

Basu, D.N. 1985. *Bangla Bhashar Bhumika*. Calcutta: Basanti Library.

Beckman, J. 1997. Positional Faithfulness, Positional Neutralization and Shona vowel harmony. *Phonology* 14: 1-46.

Chaterji, S.K. 1921. Bengali phonetics. *Bulletin of the School of Oriental Studies* 1.2: 1-25. London.

_____. 1926. *The Origin and Development of the Bengali Language*. 1971 reissue. London: George Allen & Unwin.

_____. 1928. *A Bengali Phonetic Reader*. London: University of London Press.

Chomsky, N. & M. Halle. 1968. *The Sound Pattern of English*. New York: Harper & Row.

Crothers, J. 1978. Typology and Universals of Vowel Systems. In J. Greenberb, C.A. Ferguson and E. Moravesik eds., *Unviersals of Human Language*. Vol. 2. Stanford: Stanford University Press.

Dan, M. 1992. Some Issues in Metrical Phonology of Bangla: the Indigenous Research Tradition. PhD Dissertation. Pune: Deccan College.

Das, S. 1996. Consonant Weakening in English and Bangla: a Lexical Phonological Investigation. M. Phil. Dissertation. Hyderabad: CIEFL.

Dasgupta, P. 1982. Phonology and Bangla Verb. *Indian Linguistics*. 43(1/2):17-28.

Dhar, P.C. 1977. The Segmental Phonemes of Tripura Bengali and Standard Indian English: a Comparative Study with Pedagogical Implications. M. Litt. Dissertation. Hyderabad: CIEFL.

Ghosh, T. 1996. Some Aspects of Vowel Phonology in Bangla and Bangla English. M. Phil. Dissertation. Hyderabad: CIEFL.

Hai, M. A. 1964. *Dhoni Biggan o Bangla Dhoni-Tatto*. Dhaka: Mollik Brothers.

Ito, J. 1986. *Syllable Theory in Prosodic Phonology*. New York: Garland Press.

Kager, R. 1999. *Optimality Theory*. Cambridge, UK: CUP.

Kaye, J., J. Lowenstamm and J. R. Vergnaud. 1990. Constituent Structure and Government in Phonology. *Phonology* 7: 193-231.

Kenstowicz, M. 1994. *Phonology in Generative Grammar*. Cambridge, Mass. and Oxford, UK: Blackwell.

McCarthy, J. 1979. On Stress and Syllabification. *Linguistic Inquiry* 10:443-465.

Paul, J. 1985. A Concrete Approach to Bengali Phonology. PhD Dissertation. Kanpur: IIT.

_____. 1986. Bangla Verb Morphology: a Reconstruction. *Indian Linguistics* 47, 1.4: 73-79.

Pulleyblank, D. 1993. Vowel Harmony and Optimality Theory. *Proceedings of the Workshop on Phonology* 1-18. University of Coimbra, Portugal: Associacao Portuguesa de Linguistica.

Sarkar, P. 1979. Syllable-tatto o Bangla bhasar syllable-er gathon. *Baibhab* 10:33-54.

______. 1983-84, Sarosangoti, opinihiti, obhisruti, oposruti namakaron barjoner pokkhe ekti prostab. *Bhasha* 84:50-60.

Steriade, D. 1995. Underspecification and Markedness. In J. Goldsmith ed., *The Handbook of Phonological Theory*. Oxford: Blackwell.

Selkirk, E. 1984. *Phonology and Syntax: The Relation Between Sound and Structure.* Cambridge, Mass.: MIT Press.

3

Why do the People of Tripura Speak so Fast?[1]

1.0 Introduction

Compared to binary rhythm ternary rhythm is a marked pattern of metrification attested in only a handful of world languages currently known. But of late the latter has generated a lot of heat in critical discourse on metrical phonology irrespective of the theoretical perspectives adopted by the scholars. Many proposals ensued such as TERNARY FEET (Halle and Vergnaud 1987, Levin 1988, Dresher & Lahiri 1991, Hewitt 1992, Rice 1992); binary feet with a special parsing mode called Weak Local Parsing (Hayes 1995), Relativized Extrametricality (Hammond 1990); in the Optimality Theory or OT framework, a foot-repulsion constraint *FTFT (Kager 1994). In recent times the analytical perspective on ternary rhythm has witnessed a radical change. Capitalizing on the idea that ternarity is not a primitive of metrical phonology, efforts have been made to derive ternary rhythm with binary feet through interaction of foot alignment (ALL-FT-X) with an anti-lapse constraint (Ishii 1996). However, the entire theoretical artifice is crucially dependent on an appropriate statement of the anti-lapse constraint. One such approach to define the anti-lapse constraint is the grid-based lapse constraint *LAPSE (Elenbaas 1999, Elenbaas and Kager 1999) which has proved its mettle in offering a principled and unified account of rhythmic ternarity in many a language. A welcome feature of this constraint is that it is not specific to any particular rhythm in the sense that it broadly enforces bounded rhythm, either binary or ternary.

But despite its spectacular success both empirically and typologically, *LAPSE is unable to account for the presence of a word-final triple upbeat in the trochaic system of Tripura Bangla (henceforth TB), spoken in the Indian state of Tripura. Explaining this metrical pattern requires a reformulation of the anti-lapse constraint such that only the edges of two prosodic domains - foot and word - function as valid licensors of weak beats. In this respect it differs from the earlier version conveniently renamed *LAPSE (E&K) which allows the strong beat and the word-edge to license weak beats in a grid. The main thrust of the present study is the newly defined lapse constraint *LAPSE(DE) where DE stands for *domain edges*. The advantage of *LAPSE(DE) is that it not only succeeds in accommodating the *deviant* facts of TB but also accounts for all the cross-linguistic data that provided the empirical justification to *LAPSE (E & K). Hence is the superiority of the former over the latter.

The organization of the paper is as follows. §2.0 states the metrical facts - of TB. §3.0 sketches the various theoretical approaches to ternarity: rule-based derivational approach in §3.1; early OT analysis of ternarity with the foot-repulsion constraint *FTFT (§3.2); an OT account of TB with *FTFT in §3.2.1. §4.0 presents arguments against *FTFT and introduces the anti-lapse constraint *LAPSE (§4.1). §4.2 attempts without complete success a new OT account of TB with *LAPSE. §5.0 presents a detailed argumentation for redefining the *LAPSE as *LAPSE(DE) and also demonstrates the efficacy of the new lapse constraint in predicting the facts of TB including the so called *deviant* forms in sequences of four and seven light syllables. §5.1 exemplifies the success of the new rhythmic theory in deriving the grammatical forms in Cayuvava (§ 5.1.1) and Chugach (§5.1.2) type of ternary patterns. §6.0 sums up the major findings of the study.

2.0 Facts of TB

1. TB words (containing only light syllables)

a.	zí.ra.bi	a kind of sweets'
	gó.ra.li	'ankle'
b.	bí.bɛ.sɔ.na	'consideration'
	kɛ́.ra.mo.ti	'ingenuity'
c.	pó.ri.sa.lɔ̀.na	'direction'
	ɔ́.mɔ.no.zù.gi	'inattentive'
d.	ɔ́.mɔ.no.zù.gi.ta	'inattentiveness'
	ó.nu.kɔ.rò.ni.yɔ	'imitable'
e.	ɔ́.no.nu.kɔ̀.ro.ni.yɔ	'inimitable'
f.	ɔ́.no.nu.kɔ̀.ro.ni.yɔɣ̀.ta	'inimitability'

In the TB light sequences trochees are constructed iteratively from left to right with the invariable initial primary prominence. No secondary prominence emerges in a word having less than five syllables. In the five-syllables onwards secondaries are placed on every third syllable instead of the second after the primary prominence. This results in rhythmic ternarity in longer sequences. No word-final prominence is allowed as all open syllables are underlyingly light or monomoraic and hence unable to project a foot thanks to the universal restriction against foot-degeneracy. What renders such a ternary pattern remarkable is the presence of a sequence of four weak beats or unstressed syllables at the right edge in words of length $3n+1$ i.e. four and seven syllables (cf. (lb) & (1e)). When explaining ternarity is itself a major challenge for any theory of metrical phonology, situations like these become all the more problematic. In fact there is no theory whether in the pre-OT or OT framework which can predict such a stress distribution pattern noted in TB four and seven syllables.

3.0 Different approaches to ternarity

Ternarity has been studied from various theoretical perspectives and with each theory the package of analytical apparatus has also witnessed radical changes. In the pre-OT rule based approach setting the appropriate values for relevant parameters was the decisive factor in deriving various rhythmic effects binary or ternary. In early OT, constraints were formulated to replicate the parametric values and hence not all the constraints were truly independently motivated. Recent OT mechanism therefore seeks to weed out these analytical crudities from the theory and add maximal refinements to the latter in conformity with the essential principles of the UG.

3.1 Rule-based derivational approach

The derivational approaches to ternary rhythm are characterized by proposals for various ternarity-specific analytical tools. These include TERNARY FEET (Halle & Vergnaud 1987, Levin 1988, Dresher & Lahiri 1991, Hewitt 1992, Rice 1992); Relativized Extrametricality (Hammond 1990)[2]; binary feet with a special parsing mode called Weak Local Parsing (Hayes 1995) etc. The most remarkable among these is the proposal of Hayes (1995). According to the latter analysis of rhythm - whether binary or ternary – is crucially dependent upon certain parameters and cross-linguistic variation in rhythmic patterns is the consequence of fixing particular values for these parameters. For binary rhythm these parameters include *foot type, iterativity* and *directionality.* Every language makes a selection of the appropriate *foot type* from the universal inventory - head initial (TROCHEES) or head final (IAMBS). The second parameter specifies whether foot construction is iterative or non-iterative. An iterative pattern insists on parsing maximal number of syllables into well-formed feet, which according to Hayes (1995) are always binary. Usually an unparsed syllable occupies a particular word-edge. The appropriate word-edge, which such a syllable can occupy is determined by the third parameter *directionality,* governing the direction of foot construction. For ternary rhythm an additional parameter is required namely *Foot Parsing Locality Parameter* (Hayes 1995). One of the values of this parameter is Weak Local Parsing (henceforth WLP)[3]. Selection of this parametric value forces an intervention of one unparsed syllable between two binary feet. The result is rhythmic ternarity.

In sum, the rule-based account of metrical patterns makes use of at least four parameters: *foot type, iterativity, directionality* and *foot parsing locality.* Of these, the first three are common for both binary and ternary rhythms while the fourth is specific for deriving ternary effect through spacing out of otherwise successive binary feet.

3.2 Early OT analysis of ternarity: *FTFT

In the constraint-based (i.e. Optimality Theoretic or OT) framework the first major effort at explaining ternarity is found in Kager (1994). Being an early attempt at constraint-based analysis of Cayuvava, the theoretical priorities were directed towards finding exact OT analogues for the derivational mechanisms (namely parameter setting) in the form of ranked constraints. Consequently, all the relevant constraints proposed for Cayuvava in Kager (1994) were just the metamorphosed versions of various parameters found in Hayes (1995).

2.	*Rule-based analysis*	*OT analysis*
	Extrametricality	NON-FIN (>> PARSE-σ, ALL-FT-R
	Parsing mode (WLP)	*FTFT (>> PARSE-σ)
	Iterativity	PARSE-σ, (>> ALL-FT-R)
	Directionality	ALL-FT-R (>>ALL-FT-L)

NON-FINALITY (NON-FIN) redefines extrametricality as an OT constraint, prohibiting construction of a foot on the rightmost edge of the PrWd. ALL-FT-R is the converse of ALL-FT-L, requiring feet to be maximally aligned towards the *right* edge of the PrWd. But the most important constraint for deriving ternarity is *FTFT, a counterpart of Hayesian WLP.

3. *FTFT

Feet must not be adjacent.

With these constraints and their appropriate ranking Kager (1994) demonstrates how an OT grammar for Cayuvava type ternarity can be constructed. We shall not however go into the details of these evaluation mechanisms here for which one is referred to Kager (1994), Elenbaas & Kager (1999), Das (2001). Instead we shall demonstrate how a similar OT mechanism based on the foot repulsion constraint *FTFT can perfectly predict the aspects of rhythmic ternarity noted in the light sequences of TB.

3.2.1 OT account of TB metrical pattern

Ternary rhythm in TB light sequences is the consequence of skipping one syllable every time after constructing a binary trochee. That means, TB grammar contains the following two undominated constraints.

4. FOOT BINARITY (FT-BIN)

'Feet are binary at some level of analysis (μ, σ).' (Prince and Smolensky 1993: 47)

5. TROCHEE (TROCHEE)

'Within foot, every '*' is followed by a '.'.' (Vijver 1998: 6)

Again, in every such word the head foot is aligned with the left edge. In OT terms, this requirement translates into a word-to-foot alignment constraint referring to the left edge of the word.

6. ALIGN-LEFT (ALIGN-L)

Align (PrWd-L,Ft-L) (Elenbaas and Kager 1999: 214)

Successive feet construction is prohibited under the parametric option of WLP (Weak Local Parsing) to use the Hayesian (1995) terminology. The OT counterpart of this is available in, for example, Kager (1994) in the constraint *FTFT already stated in (3) above. In a trisyllable all these constraints (3-6) are satisfied at the expense of the constraint that ensures regular iteration through exhaustive parsing namely PARSE-σ.

7. PARSE-σ

Syllables are parsed by feet.

An appropriate ranking of these constraints accounts for the optimal parse with a word initial foot in a trisyllabic word as is illustrated below.

8. *Basic constraint ranking for TB light sequences*

FT-BIN, TROCHEE, ALIGN-L, *FTFT >> PARSE-σ

9. Input: /zirabi/Optimal output: (zí.ra).bi

/zirabi/	FT-BIN	TROCHEE	ALIGN-L	*FTFT	PARSE-σ
a. (zí.ra).bi ☞				*	
b. zi.(rá.bi)			*!		*
c. (zí.ra).(bì)	*!			*	
d. (zí.rá).bi		*!			

No candidate in (9) can survive incurring a violation of any of the four undominated constraints which, having no interactions among themselves, remain unranked with each other. The optimal candidate (9a) satisfies all the undominated constraints at the cost of one violation of the lowest ranked constraint PARSE-σ. This final underparsing is in contradistinction to initial underparsing (9b). The latter is ruled out by the undominated alignment constraint ALIGN-L. The binary foot constraint comes into action in barring the candidate (9c) parsing a monosyllabic degenerate foot. This violation overshadows a more serious violation, that of the foot-repulsion constraint *FTFT. We shall see the crucial role of the latter in longer sequences where trochees are prevented from abutting each other. (9d) will never get selected in TB since feet are trochaic under all circumstance. Let us now turn to longer sequences. From now on we suppress the presence of two of the undominated constraints FT-BIN and TROCHEE in rankings.

Words of four and five syllables length do not need any new constraints. In the former (10) formation of a word-final foot through exhaustive parsing is less urgent than avoiding construction of successive feet. In a five-syllable word (11) however the need for exhaustive parsing can be satisfied to a greater degree without outraging the demands of the foot-repulsion constraint. This results in the emergence of a secondary foot aligned at the right edge. We get the first instance of iterative ternary rhythm thanks to the undominated status of *FTFT.

10. Input: /bibɛsɔna/ Optimal output: (bí.bɛ.)sɔ.na

/bibɛsɔna/	ALIGN-L	*FTFT	PARSE-σ
a. (bí.bɛ.)sɔ.na ☞			**
b. (bí.bɛ.) (sɔ.na)		*!	
c. bi.(bɛ́.sɔ.)na	*!		

11. Input: /porisalɔna/ Optimal output: (pó.ri).sa.(lɔ̀.na)

/porisalɔ.na/	ALIGN-L	*FTFT	PARSE-σ
a. (pó.ri).sa.(lɔ.na) ☞			*
b. (pó.ri).(sà.lɔ).na		*!	*
c. po.(rí.sa).(lɔ̀.na)	*!		
d. (pó.ri).sa.lɔ.na			**!*

It must have been noticed that a conflicting picture emerges in the three preceding tableaux regarding the status of extrametricality in TB. In three and four syllable words (9-10) (final) extrametricality of one and two syllables respectively is a must. But this is contradicted in a five-syllable word (11). Interestingly both these conflicting outcomes are the consequences of an identical set of constraints ranked uniformly. This is one of the beauties of OT: even a low ranked constraint can play a decisive role to evaluate the optimal candidate when the higher ranked ones fail to force a decision. This is because in OT every constraint is violable but violation must be minimal and only to satisfy the higher ranked constraints. In a trisyllable (9) evaluation of the optimal parse necessitates a minimal violation *(once)* of the lowest ranked constraint PARSE-σ to satisfy the higher ranked constraints. In a four-syllable word the minimal violation of PARSE-σ can be increased by one mark (to *two,* cf. l0a) under duress of the undominated constraints. But this is the maximal ceiling for *minimal violation* in respect of the constraint looking after maximal parsing. One extra violation mark excludes the concerned candidate from the fray. This is illustrated in the failure of the candidate (11d)

But there are occasions when even the lowest ranked constraint fails to force a decision. Such a situation arises in a six-syllable word when *two* syllables are skipped instead of *one* - the minimal number required to satisfy *FTFT - after the first foot is built. Do we then need to propose a constraint to the effect that word-medially skipping more than one syllable is prohibited? There is no such need however. For there are independently motivated edge-oriented alignment constraints like ALL-FT-X (where X refers to either the left or the right edge of the word) which keep the inter-foot distance within the *permissible* limit requiring all feet to be as close as possible to the designated edge of the PrWd.

12. ALL-FOOT-X (ALL-FT-L/R)

'The edge X of every foot coincides with the edge X of some PrWd.'

In this generalized constraint X being a variable can refer to either the left (L) or the right (R) edge of the PrWd. The relevant value of X for TB is obviously L. The demand of ALL-FT-L however is surprisingly very strong requiring the left edge of every foot to coincide with the left edge of the PrWd. Such a demand can never be satisfied in a language, which allows rhythmic alternation i.e., multiple feet within the same word: any foot other than the initial one will compulsorily violate this constraint. Obviously in TB ALL-FT-L cannot stand undominated precisely because the language displays rhythmic alternation. In fact this constraint must be dominated by PARSE-σ to enforce multiple feet per word. But though dominated by PARSE-σ, ALL-FT-L exerts its influence in a more subtle way by restricting the optimal candidate from violating it more than minimally. That is, this candidate has all its feet *as close as possible* to the left edge of the PrWd, measured by numbers of syllables distancing every foot from the left edge of the word. So the constraint ranking needed to predict the ternary alternation in a six-syllable word in TB is

13. ALIGN-L, *FTFT >> PARSE-σ >> ALL-FT-L

Interaction of these constraints is illustrated in the following tableau.

14. Input: /ɔmɔnozugita/ Optimal output: (ɔ́.mɔ).no.(zù.gi).ta

/ɔmɔnozugita/	ALIGN-L	*FTFT	PARSE-σ	ALL-FT-L
a. (ɔ́.mɔ).no.(zù.gi).ta☞			**	***
b. (ɔ́.mɔ).(nò.zu).(gì.ta)		*!*		** ****
c. ɔ.(mɔ́.no).zu.(gì.ta)	*!		**	* ****
d. (ɔ́.mɔ).no.zu.(gì.ta)			**	****!

Exclusions of candidates (14b) and (14c) from the race are self-explanatory. The critical competition is that between candidates (14a) and (14d) both of which survive the undominated constraints and score a tie on the count of PARSE-σ by carrying two violation marks each. The onus of evaluating the optimal parse then passes on to the next lower constraint in the hierarchy. Quite predictably, ALL-FT-L passes the verdict in favour of (14a) as opposed to (14d) on the strength of minimal violation.

Further evidence in support of the ranking argument PARSE-σ >> ALL-FT-L is available from the evaluation of the optimal candidate in seven-syllables. In the following tableau three candidates (15a, d, g) survive the undominated constraints and all of them fare identically with respect to the first dominated constraint namely PARSE-σ. Each has two feet and three unparsed syllables. But dis-rhythmic distribution of stresses occurs whenever inter-foot distance is more than the minimal number of syllables (i.e. *one)* needed to satisfy the higher ranked constraint *FTFT. ALL-FT-L exerting its pressure to pull the trochees maximally towards the left edge of the PrWd, then selects the candidate that minimally violates it. This candidate is (15a).

15. Input: /ɔnonukɔroniyɔ/ Optimal output: (ɔ́.no).nu.(kɔ̀.ro).ni.yɔ

/ɔnonukɔroniyɔ/	ALIGN-L	*FTFT	PARSE-σ	ALL-FT-L
a. (ɔ́.no).nu.(kɔ̀.ro).ni.yɔ ☞			***	***
b. (ɔ́.no).(nù.kɔ).(rò.ni).yɔ		*!*	*	** ****
c. (ɔ́.no).nu.(kɔ̀.ro).(nì.yɔ)		*!	*	*** *****
d. (ɔ́.no).nu.kɔ.ro.(nì.yɔ)			***	****!*
e. ɔ.(nó.nu).kɔ.(rò.ni).yɔ	*!		***	* ****
f. (ɔ́.no).nu.kɔ.(rò.ni).yɔ			***	****

Rhythmic ternarity in eight syllable words is captured straightway by the same constraint ranking. What is noticeable however is the indifferent role of ALL-FT-L in the evaluation of the optimal parse. Candidates (16b, c) are ruled out by the undominated constraints. Of the three surviving candidates (16d, e) are discounted by PARSE-σ on simple parity count. The optimal candidate has three trochees each distanced from the other by one unparsed syllable. Any more underparsing than this can be achieved only at the cost of PARSE-σ, top-ranked among the dominated constraints.

16. Input: /ɔ́nonukɔroniyɔta/ Optimal output: (ɔ́.no).nu.(kɔ̀.ro). ni.(yɔ̀.ta)

/ɔnonukɔroniyɔta/	ALIGN-L	*FTFT	PARSE-σ	ALL-FT-L
a. (ɔ́.no).nu.(kɔ̀.ro). ni (yɔ̀.ta) ☞			**	*** *****
b. (ɔ́.no).(nù.kɔ). (rò.ni).(yɔ̀.ta)		*!**		** **** *****
c. ɔ.(nó.nu).kɔ. (rò.ni).yɔ.ta	*!		***	* ****
d. (ɔ́.no).nu.kɔ.ro. (nì.yɔ).ta			***!*	*****
e. (ɔ́.no).nu.kɔ. (rò.ni).yɔ.ta			***!*	****

So far we have seen that a simple constraint ranking FT-BIN, TROCHEE, ALIGN-L, *FTFT >> PARSE-σ >> ALL-FT-L accounts for all types of light sequences in TB. Rhythmic ternarity is primarily the consequence of the undominated foot-repulsion constraint *FTFT spacing out the trochees towards the right, the direction of alternation. The opposite edge alignment constraint ALL-FT -L however sees to it that the trochees do not travel far away from the left edge, more than the distance needed to satisfy *FTFT in terms of number of syllables. The word-final double underparsing in words of length $3n+1$ (i.e., four and seven) syllables is due to the joint effects of undominated FT-BIN and *FTFT.

4.0 Arguing against *FTFT and introducing *LAPSE

But despite this neat picture of the metrical analysis of ternarity in TB, one cannot but express a strong reservation against it and in this respect the arguments against the existence of the foot-repulsion constraint *FTFT put forward in Elenbaas and Kager (1999) are worth adhering to. It is obvious that this constraint has to be replaced with a more natural and independently motivated one. This is because ternarity is not a primitive in the metrical systems of the world languages as because it is attested in only very few languages. Analysis of ternarity therefore should not necessitate a ternarity-specific constraint; but rather should follow from the interaction of more general constraints responsible for rhythmic effects universally. Moreover purpose-specificity as a characteristic of a constraint, which is by definition universal and maximally generalized, is counterintuitive especially since all constraints are supposedly parts of UG. Finally, being specific to ternarity *FTFT remains as good as any ternarity-specific analytical device proposed in the rule-base approach such as TERNARY FEET, WLP, or Relativized Extrametricality etc. The next issue to address therefore is how to find out a suitable alternative to *FTFT.

4.1 OT grammar of *LAPSE

Efforts have been made in recent OT analyses to eliminate this ternarity-specific canstraint and to suggest alternative methods of capturing ternarity. Most prominent among these are Ishii (1996) and Elenbaas and Kager (1999). It was Ishii who first suggested the idea that ternarity arises from the interaction of foot alignment constraints (ALL-FT-X) with an anti-lapse constraint. Assuming Kager (1994) Ishii proposes an antilapse constraint PARSE-2[4] that stipulates that 'of every two stress units one must be parsed into a foot'. But such a formulation engenders serious complications and more often than not fails to deliver the goods. (For details see Elenbaas and Kager (1999).

Consequently, Elenbaas and Kager (1999) propose a new anti-lapse constraint *LAPSE.

17. *LAPSE

. Every weak beat must be adjacent to a strong beat or the word-edge.

Based on the *Anti-lapse Provision* of Selkirk (1984)[5], *LAPSE does not involve any counting of weak beats. This absolutely rhythmic constraint is based on the notion of licensing. Explaining this aspect of *LAPSE, Elenbaas and Kager (1999: 282) write:

> "All that *LAPSE does is to check the linear adjacency of a weak beat with respect to rhythmic landmarks: either a strong beat or an edge. In this view, strong beats and edges become the LICENSORS of weak beats."

In brief, a weak beat which is neither adjacent to a strong beat nor to a word-edge violates *LAPSE. Superiority of *LAPSE as opposed to its OT predecessor *FTFT lies in that it is not aimed at generating any particular rhythmic effect. It only ensures rhythmic alternation by prohibiting long sequences of weak beats. What should be the nature of the rhythm — binary or ternary — is the consequence of interaction of other constraints particularly the various alignment constraints ALL-FT-X, ALIGN-Y etc. with *LAPSE. Elenbaas and Kager (1999) successfully apply *LAPSE to provide a unified account to various ternary patterns - regular as well as occasional — noted in different languages. Let us now apply the same to explain the stress distribution pattern of TB light sequences.

4.2 Applying *LAPSE to TB metrics

TB light sequences of three to eight syllables (maximum size of a non-compound word) can be classified into three subtypes: words of length $3n$ (i.e. three and six syllables), $3n+1$ (i.e. four and seven syllables), and $3n+2$ (i.e. five and eight syllables). Our effort in this section is to construct an OT grammar that accounts for each of these subtypes. To start with let us see what constraints are needed for the purpose in addition to *LAPSE.

The core constraint ranking for generating ternarity effect in any language is as in (18).

18. *LAPSE >> ALL-FT-X >> PARSE-σ (Elenbaas and Kager 1999, Das 2001).

This constraint ranking can be interpreted in the following way. If in a particular language the underparsing constraint ALL-FT-X overrides the demand for exhaustive parsing of syllables signified by the constraint PARSE-σ, unbounded system will result with only one foot standing at the designated edge (left or right) of the PrWd. But the force of the underparsing constraint is cut to size if the anti-lapse constraint *LAPSE dominates it. Since *LAPSE does not allow more than two weak beats in between two strong beats or a strong beat and the adjacent word-edge, every strong beat can be followed or preceded by maximally two weak beats or unparsed syllables (assuming no syllable weight distinction). The result is ternary rhythm.

In this new OT analysis of ternarity, directionality of footing is the consequence of which of the two underparsing constraints — ALL-FT-L or ALL-FT-R — figures predominantly in the constraint hierarchy. In a language like TB where foot construction begins at the left edge of the PrWd and proceeds towards the right, ALL-FT-R dominates over ALL-FT-L. The latter, though dominated, exerts a subtle counter pressure to pull the trochees towards the left and in consequence of this tension of the two opposing forces the maximal inter-foot distance remains within the limit of one (unparsed) syllable. Dominance of ALL-FT -L over PARSE-σ is justified by the absence of persistent footing in TB. Beside these in TB every word begins with a foot (a trochee). This motivates the invocation of the undominated word-to-foot alignment constraint ALIGN-L. Assuming the undominated presence of the two constraints FT-BIN (4) and TROCHEE (5) (suppressed in the ranking) we therefore have evidence to construct the following constraint ranking for explaining ternarity in TB.

19. *LAPSE, ALIGN-L >> ALL-FT-R >> ALL-FT-L >> PARSE-σ[6]

We first illustrate the efficacy of this ranking in respect of TB words of 3*n* syllables.

20. Input: /zirabi/Optimal output: (zí.ra).bi

/zirabi/	*LAPSE	ALIGN-L	ALL-FT-R	ALL-FT-L	PARSE-σ
a. (zí.ra).bi☞			*		*
b. zi.(rá.bi)		*!		*	*

Trisyllables present the simplest instances of ternarity without of course making the effects of rhythmic alternation obvious. Any way, the prediction of the revised constraint hierarchy built on the basis of the findings of E&K and using the undominated anti-lapse constraint *LAPSE, is proved perfectly accurate in evaluating the optimal parse. Rhythmic ternarity however is clearly attested in the other member of the 3*n* subtype i.e. six-syllables.

21. Input: /ɔmɔnozugita/ Optimal output: (ɔ́.mɔ).no.(zù.gi).ta

/ɔmɔnozugita/	*LAPSE	ALIGN-L	ALL-FT-R	ALL-FT-L	PARSE-σ
a. (ɔ́.mɔ).no. (zù.gi).ta ☞			* ****	***	**
b. (ɔ́.mɔ). (nò.zu). (gí.ta)			** ****!	** ****	

c. ɔ.(mɔ́.no). zu.(gì.ta)		*!	***	* ****	**
d. (ɔ́.mɔ).no.zu. (gì.ta)	*!		** ****	**	**
e. (ɔ́.m̩ɔ). (nò.zu).gi.ta	*!		** ****	**	**
f. (ɔ́.mɔ).no. zu.gi.ta	*!**		****		****

Only two candidates (21a, b) survive the undominated constraints. Of these (21b) is ruled out by the high ranking underparsing constraint ALL-FT-R as the former violates the latter *maximally* (i.e. as opposed to *minimally*) by constructing one extra foot in excess of what is minimally required to satisfy the anti-lapse constraint *LAPSE. In other words, the spacing-out effect that causes ternarity in (21a) is obstructed in (21b) due to the dense parsing of syllables in the latter, resulting in perfect binarity. Initial underparsing is always at the cost of fatal violation of undominated alignment requirement of ALIGN-L. This explains the suboptimality of (21c). All the three remaining candidates (21d-f) incur one or more fatal violations of *LAPSE and hence are excluded. Whenever there is a sequence of more than two weak beats the medial one will lack a licensor whether in the form of a strong beat (21d) or word-edge (21e). We have shown the erring beat (syllable) marked as underlined. By the same calculation there are three unlicensed weak beats in a sequence of five in (21f).

We now apply the constraint hierarchy (19) to evaluate the grammatical forms in words of length $3n+2$ syllables. Generally the minimum number of feet required for a word of $3n+2$ syllables equals n. In other words, in a word of five syllables the minimum number of feet expected is *one* and in a word of eight syllables the number is *two.* But what we notice in reality in TB is the excess presence of one syllable in both the cases. What could be the factor enforcing such an additional foot in such type of words? To find the desired answer let us look at the following tableaux.

22. Input: /porisalɔna/ Optimal output: (pó.ri).sa.(lɔ̀.na)

/porisalɔna/	*LAPSE	ALIGN-L	ALL-FT-R	ALL-FT-L	PARSE-σ
a. (pó.ri).sa .(lɔ̀.na) ☞			***	***	*
b. (pó.ri). (sà.lɔ).na			* ***!	**	*
c. po.(rí.sa). (lɔ̀.na)		*!	**	***	*
d. (pò.ri). sa.lɔ.na	*!*		***		***

In (22) three candidates (a, b, c) contain two feet each i.e., one in excess of what is required for a word of $3n+2$ (i.e. five) syllables. In contrast, (22d) conforms to the minimum figure of one foot. But surprisingly it is the *deviant* forms with two feet which satisfy the undominated anti-lapse constraint *LAPSE whereas the *ideal* form (22d) incurs two fatal violation of the said constraint. The question that has been troubling us so far is now well answered: undominated *LAPSE does not tolerate a sequence of more than two weak beats. Consequently it enforces one extra stress, and hence an extra foot, for its own satisfaction. Any candidate having less than two feet in a five-syllable word is thus ruled out by *LAPSE. Out of three candidates that survive *LAPSE, (22c) is thrown out by the undominated ALIGN-L. Only two candidates (22a-b) now remain in the fray and the judgment passes on to the constraint standing immediately below the undominated ones as both these remaining candidates fare identically in respect of the latter. Perfect binarity occurs in (22b) due to the fact that both the feet are pushed maximally leftwards incurring one extra violation of right edge oriented constraint ALL-FT-R compared to the ternary rhythm candidate (22a). ALL-FT-R then gives the verdict in favour of (22a) vindicating the minimality condition of violation - one of the key principles in OT. The same explanation is repeated in the success story of the most harmonic candidate (23a) in an eight-syllable word excepting that here the number of feet increases by one more.

23. Input: /ɔnonukɔroniyɔta/ Optimal output: (ɔ́.no).nu.(kɔ̀.ro). ni.(yɔ̀.ta)

/ɔnonukɔroniyɔta/	*LAPSE	ALIGN-L	ALL-FT-R	ALL-FT-L	PARSE-σ
a. (ɔ́.no).nu. (kɔ̀.ro).ni.(yɔ̀.ta) ☞			*** ******	*** ******	**
b. (ɔ́.no).(nù.kɔ). (rò.ni).(yɔ́.ta)			** **** ****! **	** **** ******	
c. ɔ.(nó.nu).kɔ. (rò.ni).yɔ.ta	*!	*	** *****	* ****	****
d. (ɔ́.no).nu.kɔ. ro.(nì.yɔ).ta	*!*		* ******	*****	****
e. (ɔ́.no).nu.kɔ. (rò.ni).yɔ.ta	*!*		** ******	****	****
f. (ɔ́.no).(nù.kɔ). (rò.ni).yɔ.ta	*!		** **** ******	** ****	**

It is time now to look at the third and last subtype of TB words which equal a length of $3n+1$ (i.e. four and seven) syllables. An interesting thing happens here posing a serious challenge to the efficacy of constraint ranking (19) which has so far yielded the desired results in predicting ternarity in TB. Let us first consider two representative words of the specified length.

24. a. (bí.bɛ).<u>sɔ</u>.na 'consideration'
b. (ɔ́.no).nu.(kɔ̀.ro).<u>ni</u>.yɔ 'inimitable'

In both these words three weak beats follow the rightmost strong beat. Going by the current definition of the anti-lapse constraint, *LAPSE, as proposed by Elenbaas and Kager (1999), both of them incur one fatal violation each by having an unlicensed weak beat (marked with underline). The optimal forms predicted by the OT grammar (19) in respect of words of this subtype thus severely contradict the attested facts of the language. The following tableaux are presented for illustration.

25. Input: /bibɛsɔna/ Optimal output: (bî.bɛ.)sɔ.na

/bibɛsɔna/	*LAPSE	ALIGN-L	ALL-FT-R	ALL-FT-L	PARSE-σ
a. (bí.bɛ).sɔ.na	*!		**		**
b. (bí.bɛ).(sɔ̀.na) ☞?		**	**		
c. bi.(bɛ́.sɔ).na		*!	*	*	**

26. Input: /ɔnonukɔroniyɔ/ Optimal output: (ɔ́.no).nu.(kɔ̀.ro). (ní.yɔ)

/ɔnonukɔroniyɔ/	*LAPSE	ALIGN-L	ALL-FT-R	ALL-FT-L	PARSE-σ
a. (ɔ́.no).nu. (kɔ̀.ro).ni.yɔ	*!		** *****		***
b. (ɔ́.no).(nù.kɔ). (rò.ni).yɔ			* *** ****!*	** ****	*
c. (ɔ́.no).nu .(kɔ̀.ro). (ní.yɔ) ☞?			** *****	*** *****	*
d. (ɔ́.no).nu. kɔ.ro.(nì.yɔ)	*!*		*****	*****	***
e. ɔ.(nó.nu).kɔ. (rò.ni).yɔ		*!	* ****	* ****	***
f. (ɔ́.no).nu. kɔ.(rò.ni).yɔ	*!		* *****	****	***

The optimal parses (25b) and (26c) display binary rhythm with only local ternarity in the latter. By contrast the desired optimal candidates, which attest regular ternarity (25a) and (26a) are excluded by incurring one fatal violation each on the count of the anti-lapse constraint.

The real problem confronting us is what sort of constraint ranking is capable of providing a uniform account for all the three subtypes of words in TB. Or more precisely, is it really the problem of reorganizing the constraint ranking or redefining some of the constraints? We shall argue (in the following section) that it is not any reorganization of the constraint ranking but an appropriate statement of the undominated anti-lapse constraint *LAPSE that holds the key to the solution of the problem.

5.0 TB metrics and an argument for redefining *LAPSE

In terms of the core grammar proposed in Elenbaas and Kager (1999) for generating ternarity, *LAPSE must remain undominated in the hierarchy. This is because the purpose of this constraint is to ban long sequences of weak beats. Domination of *LAPSE and PARSE-σ by the underparsing constraints ALL-FT-X will produce unbounded systems. Conversely when *LAPSE and PARSE-σ dominate ALL-FT-X, binary rhythm results[7]. As far as ternarity is concerned it is ensured only by the ranking *LAPSE >> ALL-FT–X >> PARSE-σ. These typological predictions are based on the findings of Elenbaas and Kager (1999).

27. a. ALL-FT-X >> PARSE-σ, *LAPSE (unbounded system)

b. *LAPSE, PARSE-σ >> ALL-FT-X (binary system)

c. *LAPSE >> ALL-FT-X >> PARSE-σ (ternary system)

It is obvious therefore that for ternarity *LAPSE must dominate ALL-FT-X >> PARSE-σ and this has been sufficiently evidenced in the evaluation of ternarity in TB words of lengths $3n$ and $3n+2$ (cf. 20-23). In other words constraint reranking does not hold the answer for the elimination of binary rhythm in words of length $3n+1$.

Let us now consider the other possibility: constraint redefining. The constraint that plays the all-important role of ruling out final triple upbeat in words of length 3n+1 syllables is the anti-lapse constraint *LAPSE. In the absence of it, the evaluation would have passed on to one of the edge-oriented alignment constraints ALL-FT-L because both the non-trivial candidates i.e. (a) & (b) in (25) and (a) & (c) in (26) score a tie in respect of ALL-FT-R and incur no violation on the count of the word-to-foot alignment constraint ALIGN-L. The verdict of ALL-FT-L goes in favour of the desired candidates i.e. the ones with final triple upbeat for the simple reason of minimal violations on parity count. So, if any constraint needs to be restated for accommodating the facts of TB in terms of the present ranking, it must be the anti-lapse constraint, *LAPSE.

As per its current definition, 'Every weak beat must be adjacent to a strong beat or the word-edge' (Elenbaas and Kager 1999: 282), only stresses and word-edges can license a weak beat. In other words the distance between two licensors should not be more than two weak beats so that each licensor has one (the maximal number allowed) weak beat within its licensing scope. Facts of TB however demand that the licensing scope of at least one of these prosodic categories[8] should be extended to include *two* weak beats so that a sequence of triple upbeat can be easily accommodated. Now the question arises, which one of these licensors should enjoy this benefit of extended scope? If every strong beat were permitted to license two weak beats each, then there would arise a pattern in which inter-stress distance would be maximized to four weak beats! No metrical system is currently known in which rhythmic alternation involves such a quaternary distribution of stress. The focus then shifts to the other licensor i.e. word-edge. But which word-edge? If both the edges of a word were allowed to license two weak beats each, there is a possibility of having as many as six weak beats[9] within a single word with just one stress. To achieve a semblance of rhythmic effect at all, with such a large number of weak beats, every word must have an overlong size, a phenomenon very rare in natural languages. Implication for the theory therefore is that the extra licensing facility should be restricted to only one of the edges of word, either initial or final. Doing this involves the danger of reintroducing the provision of parametric options in OT. This would be a bizarre situation given the avowed renunciation of any parametric options by OT. The latter instead constructs grammar on the basis of interactions of universal violable constraints.

To get round this array of complications it would be worthwhile to consider the possibility of projecting foot-edge as a valid licensor of weak beats[10]. Once again such a proposition is fraught with the danger of increasing the number of weak beats in a word if both the edges of a foot are accepted as valid licensors in the same language. Empirically, every language selects a particular foot-edge as licensor of a weak beat. Selection of this particular foot-edge however is not subject to any parametric selection. This is ensured if directionality of iteration is taken into consideration. The licensing edge of the foot must coincide with the direction of footing. That is, *if rhythmic footing proceeds from left to right, only the right edge of a foot can license a weak beat. Conversely, if the alternation were directed towards the left, the left edge of the foot would be the licensor. This is independent of any distinction of foot-dominance. Let us call this licensing foot-edge* ***directional foot-edge***. It is a separate issue how directionality is captured in terms a constraint hierarchy. We shall get back to that before long.

But once again this is too strong a proposition. For if in a word with multiple feet every foot allows one weak beat through *directional foot-edge* licensing, the optimal candidate in a six-syllable word with trochaic feet, will have a regular sequence of three upbeats word-medially since the following strong beat will also license a weak beat on either of its side. That is, in a language with left-to-right trochaic pattern a word of six syllables will have a metrical pattern like (σ́σ)σσ(σ̀σ) instead of (σ́σ)σ(σ̀σ)σ. The former scansion with a medial triple upbeat produces a quaternary pattern while the latter with a medial double upbeat yields a perfectly ternary rhythm. That the ternary pattern is a cross-linguistically favoured one is established by the following examples from languages representing both iambic and trochaic systems.

28.

a. (à.ri).hi.(hî.be).e	vs.	*(à.ri.)hi.hi.(bé.e)	(Cayuvava)	R→L[11]
b. (á.ku).tar. (tù.nir).tuq	vs.	*(à.ku).tar.tu. (nir.tùq)	(Chugach)	L→R
c. (pú.he).li. mìs.ta).ni	vs.	*(pú.he).li.mis. (tà.ni)	(Finnish)	L→R

d. (ó.sa).va.(mà.le).ki vs. *(ó.sa).va.ma.(lè.ki) (Estonian) L→R

e. (ɔ́.mɔ).no.(zù.gi).ta vs. *(ɔ́.mɔ).no.zu.(gì.ta) (TB) L→R

The net result of the above discussion supported by cross-linguistic evidence is that the directional edge of all feet is not entitled to become the licensor of a weak beat. The question then arises what types of feet are allowed to employ their directional edge as licensor of weak beats. Insights from the preceding discussion tell us that it is (only) the iteration-final directional foot-edge that can license a weak beat. In a trochaic language like TB with alternation proceeding from left to right, this weak beat licensed by the iteration-final directional foot-edge is flanked by one more on each side: it is preceded by the one licensed by the immediately preceding strong beat and is followed by the one licensed by the following word-edge. This gives the *problematic* sequence of three weak beats word-finally in TB words containing four and seven syllables.

In the wake of this discovery of a third type of licensor for weak beats in a word, an appropriate restatement of the anti-lapse constraint is well warranted.

29. *New anti-lapse constraint* (pre-final version)

*LAPSE

> Every weak beat must be adjacent to a strong beat or the iteration-final foot-edge or a word-edge.

The licensing effects of all these three prosodic units mentioned in the definition of *LAPSE unite together to give a cumulative result of a triple upbeat word-finally (cf. TB).

But if examined critically, this newly defined *LAPSE turns out to be highly nonrestrictive compared to its predecessor, which we from now on refer to as *LAPSE (E&K): the former has three clauses, each contributing a licensor while the latter has only two. The greater descriptive adequacy noticed in the new *LAPSE (29), is only at the cost of economy of generalizations. It is worthwhile therefore to explore the possibility of reducing the number of clauses incorporated in the new anti-lapse constraint.

The careful reader must have noticed that while defining the *directional foot-edge* as a licensor of weak beats we have made no reference to foot-dominance. This is because in deciding the licensing edge of a foot, its head or the strong beat plays no role at all. In fact, given that in a ternary rhythm only one syllable remains unparsed in between two feet and that this unparsed syllable (or weak beat) now has a licensor in either of the foot-edges adjacent to it, the licensing scope of a strong beat logically gets reduced to the foot internal domain. If a strong beat is allowed to license a weak beat outside the domain of foot, every weak beat standing outside the domain of a foot and also away from the licensing scope of a word-edge, will be subject to double licensing by either of the adjacent foot-edges as well as the adjacent strong beat. Such a provision for double licensing stands contrary to the principle of economy.

It then follows that in terms of the redefined *LAPSE (29) the role of a strong beat as a licensor for weak beats is a very restricted one, confined only to licensing the foot internal weak beat. But is it not sheer redundancy to make provision for licensing a foot internal weak beat through a separate constraint? Any constraint hierarchy having undominated FT-BIN (stipulating that feet are binary) and TROCHEE or FT=IAMB (specifying the relevant foot-type), accounts for the fact that within a foot every weak beat stands adjacent to a strong beat. It is unnecessary therefore to project a separate constraint for a purpose, which is already taken care of by other constraints.

In sum, there is no justification for incorporating the clause mentioning the strong beat as one of the licensors of weak beats in a maximally restrictive statement of the antilapse constraint. Let us therefore revise the definition of the concerned constraint and distinguish it from now onwards as *LAPSE (DE) where the bracketed abbreviation DE stands for *Domain Edge:* foot and word are established prosodic domains.

30. *LAPSE (DE)

Every weak beat must be adjacent either to a *directional foot-edge* or word-edge.

Before we go on to show how this new constraint functions in a constraint hierarchy and accounts for the facts of TB and also of other languages, a word about the factors determining the licensing edge of a foot is worth the while. We have seen earlier that directionality of footing is generally taken care of by the two edge-oriented alignment constraints ALL-FT-R and ALL-FT-L. In course of performing their normal duty of pulling the binary feet towards the respective edge of the PrWd represented by the values for R/L (i.e. right/left), these constraints indicate the direction of alternation. In our new approach to ternarity also these edge-oriented alignment constraints perform the same function. But in addition they also play a crucial role in determining the licensing edge of a foot, which is dependent on the directionality of iteration. In a constraint ranking where ALL-FT-R is ranked high and undominated by any other alignment constraint, the foot edge capable of licensing a weak beat will be the right edge. In the converse situation where its left edge counterpart holds the sway, iteration will run towards the left and the left edge of every foot would license a weak beat.

But very often these edge-oriented alignment constraints are dominated by either of the word-to-foot alignment constraints ALIGN-L or ALIGN-R or both. The question to ask then is how does the constraint ranking determine the direction of footing and in consequence the licensing edge of a foot. In terms of the new OT mechanism that we propose here to account for rhythmic ternarity, direction of iteration falls out automatically from the highest ranked of the four alignment constraints: ALIGN-L & ALIGN-R and ALL-FT-L & ALL-FT-R. We have already mentioned that the edge-oriented alignment constraints ALL-FT-L & ALL-FT-R indicate that the direction of footing coincides with the value represented by L or R in the respective constraints. But the word-to-foot alignment constraints ALIGN-L & ALIGN-R suggest that footing proceeds opposite to the direction implied by the value of L or R. That is, if ALIGN-L ranks highest among the alignment constraints, iteration proceeds towards the opposite edge i.e. towards the *right.* On the contrary, if ALIGN-R tops the list, foot construction proceeds towards the *left.*

Automatically, in the former case the *right* edge of a foot functions as the licensor of an adjacent weak beat; and conversely, in the latter case, the *directional foot-edge* capable of licensing a weak beat is the *left* edge. Now, more often than not, these word-to-foot alignment constraints remain undominated in the overall constraint hierarchy of a language and in this respect they differ from the edge-oriented alignment constraints. The reason for this however is not difficult to find. ALIGN-X demands that the left or right edge of *one* foot must be aligned with the corresponding edge of some PrWd. Very often this foot stands out from the rest as the head-foot in the PrWd. Such constraints therefore impose strict alignment and (may) remain undomainated (either one or both) in the hierarchy. When both ALIGN-L & ALIGN-R are undominated iteration becomes bidirectional and both the edges, *left* and *right,* of the foot become licensors: i.e. *left* edge of the right aligned foot and *right* edge of the left aligned foot (cf. Sentani in Elenbaas and Kager 1999, Das 2001)[12]. Contrary to ALIGN constraints, ALL-FT-X can never remain undominated because it is practically impossible to have *all* the feet of a word aligned with a particular edge of the PrWd. Consequently, in any language which allows rhythmic alternation, and hence multiple feet per word, ALL-FT-X functions as a gradient constraint whose violation is counted in terms of the number of syllables separating the feet from the designated edge of the PrWd. In the absence of ALIGN-X, the highest ranked All-FT-X determines the direction of alternation and hence the licensing edge of a foot. The following algorithm sums up the entire story behind deciding the directional foot-edge and hence the licensing edge of a foot.

(31)

i) Locate the highest ranking member of the set of four foot-alignment constraints

(ALIGN-L, ALIGN-R, ALL-FT-L, ALL-FT-R).

ii) If it is ALIGN-L, then the directional foot-edge, (i.e. the licensing edge) is the opposite i.e. right. If it is ALIGN-R, then the directional foot-edge (hence the licensing edge) is left.

iii) But if it is ALL-FT-L, then the directional foot-edge is left. If it is ALL-FT-R, then the directional foot-edge is right.

iv) If both ALIGN-L and ALIGN-R are tied at the top of the ranking, then both the edge of every foot can license a weak beat (resulting in bi-directional footing).

Finally, it should be clearly understood that in this new approach, no alignment constraint is entrusted with the responsibility of licensing weak beats (whether one or more). Licensing is the sole responsibility of the anti-lapse constraint *LAPSE (DE) which specifically mentions the two eligible licensors: *directional foot-edge* and word-edge. In respect of licensing, the role of the alignment constraints is at the most indirect. They only determine – depending on which among them top(s) the list – the direction of foot construction and, by implication, the particular edge of a foot capable of licensing a weak beat. Determination of the other licensor i.e. word-edge is automatic and follows from its linear adjacency to the licensor.

We shall now demonstrate how the new anti-lapse constraint (30) accounts for the deviant forms in TB (cf. 24). We continue to suppress the presence of the undominated constraints FT-BIN and TROCHEE in the ranking.

(32) Input: /bibɛsɔna/ Optimal output: (bí.bɛ.)sɔ.na

/bibɛsɔna/	*LAPSE (DE)	ALIGN-L	ALL-FT-R	ALL-FT-L	PARSE-σ
a. (bí.bɛ). sɔ.na ☞			**		**
b. (bí.bɛ). (sɔ̀.na)			**	*!*	
c. bi.(bɛ́.sɔ). na		*!	*	*	**

As stated earlier, ALIGN-L, being the highest of the alignment constraints in the hierarchy, points out that footing proceeds from left to right and that the *right* edge of the foot licenses a weak beat. That is, in the optimal parse in (32a) of the three word-final weak beats the foot internal weak beat bɛ is taken care of by undominated constraints FT-BIN and TROCHEE. The second weak beat sɔ is licensed by the *directional foot edge* i.e. the *right* edge of the foot. And the last weak beat represented by the syllable na finds its licensor in the adjacent (*right*) edge of the word. Consequently, no violation is attested in respect of the anti-lapse constraint *LAPSE (DE) for the candidate (32a) which has been excluded by *LAPSE (E&K). The critical competition is between candidates (32a) and (32b). Both survive the undominated constraints and are logged in a tie in respect of ALL-FT-R. Quite expectedly the charge of evaluation shifts to the next constraint down the hierarchy ALL-FT-L and the latter rules in favour of (32a) on consideration of minimal violation. This justifies our claim that in the presence of highest-ranking ALIGN-X, which determines the licensing edge as well as direction of iteration, the role of edge-oriented alignment constraint ALL-FT-X is only to mark the distance of the feet of the candidates from the respective edge of the PrWd and judge the optimal candidate on parity count.

The selection of the optimal candidate (33a) for a seven syllable word in the following tableau repeats the same story with the difference that owing to the increased number of potential candidates we can see here the crucial role of *LAPSE (DE) in action.

33. Input: /ɔnonukɔroniyɔ/ Optimal output: (ɔ́.no).nu.(kɔ̀.ro). (nì.yɔ)

/ɔnonukɔroniyɔ/	*LAPSE (DE)	ALIGN-L	ALL-FT-R	ALL-FT-L	PARSE-σ
a. (ɔ́.no).nu.(kɔ̀.ro). ni.yɔ ☞			** *****		***
b. (ɔ́.no).(nù.kɔ). (rò.ni).yɔ			* *** ****!*	** ****	*

c. (ɔ́.no).nu.(kɔ̀.ro).(nì.yɔ)			** *****	*** *!****	*
d. (ɔ́.no).nu.kɔ.ro .(nì.yɔ)	*!*		*****	*****	***
e. ɔ.(nó.nu).kɔ.(rò.ni).yɔ		*!	* ****	* ****	***
f. (ɔ́.no).nu.kɔ.(rò.ni).yɔ	*!		* *****	****	***

Perfect ternary rhythm occurs in (33a) owing to the presence of three weak beats following the secondary stress. All the three weak beats have their respective licensors and are therefore approved of by the new anti-lapse constraint *LAPSE (DE). Its closest rival (33c), which would have been chosen optimal by *LAPSE (E&K), is also passed by *LAPSE (DE). But (33c) is excluded because of its having an additional foot (formed 'persistently' on the last two syllables) incurring non-minimal violations of the left-edge oriented alignment constraint ALL-FT-L. (33b) instantiates perfect binarity thanks to its maximally dense parsing. It thus incurs more violations than necessary on the count of the high ranking underparsing constraint ALL-FT-R requiring the trochees to be maximally close to the right edge of the PrWd. The 'hammock' pattern in (33d) is ruled against because out of its four inter-stress weak beats the rightmost two (in underline) lack licensors. (33f) repeats the same story with the variation that here only one weak beat goes unlicensed at the fatal expense of the anti-lapse constraint. Undominated word-to-foot alignment constraint ALIGN-L rules out candidate (33e) owing to the misalignment displayed by the latter between the left edge of its initial foot and the left edge of the PrWd.

In sum, in this section we have seen that the rhythmic theory of anti-lapse can be improved substantially to accommodate the *un predicted* metrical realities of TB by redefining the crucial anti-lapse constraint. The revised version of the relevant constraint named

*LAPSE (DE), as opposed to its predecessor conveniently renamed *LAPSE (E&K), discards strong beat as a licensor of weak beats and introduces *directional foot edge* as a new licensor. Advantage of this revised constraint is that it explains all the so-called *deviant* forms in TB. In the next section we extend our OT account of ternarity to some other languages to show its efficacy across languages.

5.1 Extending the new rhythmic theory to other ternary systems

To demonstrate the cross-linguistic applicability of the new theory of rhythmicity based on the reformulated lapse constraint *LAPSE (DE) I present illustrations from two languages Cayuvava and Chugach which exhibit regular ternarity[13].

Cayuvava

Cayuvava is an iterative trochaic system with ternary rhythm. Main stress falls on the antepenult and alternation moves from right to left. Persistent footing[14] is not allowed. To illustrate how the new anti-lapse constraint *LAPSE (DE) produces the desired results we present the following tableaux for six, seven and eight syllables. The erring beats (or syllables) on the count of *LAPSE (DE) are underlined. The OT ranking for Cayuvava is

34. *LAPSE (DE) >> ALL-FT-L >> ALL-FT-R >> PARSE-σ

35. Input: /arihihibee/ Optimal form: (à.ri).hi.(hí.be).e

/arihihibee/	*LAPSE (DE)	ALL-FT-L	ALL-FT-R	PARSE-σ
a. (à.ri).hi.hi.be.e	*!**		****	****
b. a.ri.(hì.hi).be.e	*!	**	**	****
c. (á.ri).(hì.hi).be.e	*!	**	** ****	**
d. (á.ri).hi.(hì.be).e ☞		***	* ****	**
e. (á.ri).hi.hi.(bè.e)	*!	****	****	**
f. a.(rî.hi).hi.(bè.e)		* ***!*	***	**
g. (á.ri).(hì.hi).(bè.e)		** **!**	** ****	

According to our new proposition, in (35) the highest ranked of the alignment constraints ALL-FT-L determines that footing proceeds from right to left and by implication, that the licensing edge of a foot is the *left* edge. Thus a weak beat abutting the left edge of a foot is duly licensed. By contrast a weak beat standing on the right edge of a foot stands unlicensed, so to speak, unless it is adjacent to a word-edge. All the underlined weak beats stand on the right side of a foot and all, excepting the word-final one, lack a licensor (cf. 35a-c). In (35e) of the two medial unparsed syllables the first one *hi* cannot be licensed by the preceding foot since the licensing edge of a foot is *left* edge. Contrary to this the following unparsed syllable (weak beat) *hi* is licensed by the *left* edge of the following foot. All these four candidates are ruled against by *LAPSE (DE). Of the remaining candidates (35f-g) are excluded as they incur non-minimal violations in respect of ALL-FT-L. (35d) satisfies the anti-lapse constraint *LAPSE (DE) and has the least number of violations permitted by the higher ranked constraints and wins the fray. The same principles of stress assignment are at work in evaluating the most harmonic candidate in the following two tableaux in (36-37) for seven and eight syllables respectively. We do not go into the details of the evaluation processes of individual candidates, which should be self-explanatory.

36. Input: /marahahaeiki/Optimal output: ma.(rà.ha)ha.(é.i).ki

/marahahaeiki/	*LAPSE (DE)	ALL-FT-L	ALL-FT-R	PARSE-σ
a. (má.ra).ha. ha.e.i.ki	*!***		*****	*****
b. ma.ra.(háha).e.i.ki	*!*	**	***	*****
c. ma.(rà.ha).ha. (é.i).ki ☞		* ****	* ****	***
d. ma.ra.(hà.ha).(é.i).ki		** ****!	* ***	***
e. ma.ra.(hà.ha).e.(í.ki)		** ****!*	***	***
f. (mà.ra).ha.(há.e).i.ki	*!	***	** *****	***
g. (mà.ra).(hà.ha).(é.i).ki		** ****!	* *** *****	*

37. Input: /ikitaparerepeha/ Optimal output: i.ki.(tà.pa).re .(ré.pe).ha

/ikitaparerepeha/	*LAPSE (DE)	ALL-FT-L	ALL-FT-R	PARSE-σ
a. i.(kì.ta).pa.(ré.re). <u>pe</u>.ha	*!	* ****	** *****	****
b. i.ki.(tà.pa).re. (ré.pe).ha ☞		** *****	* ****	****
c. (ì.ki).(tà.pa).re. (ré.pe).ha		** *****	* **** *! *****	**
d. (ì.ki).ta.(pà.re). re.(pé.ha)		*** *****!*	*** ******	**
e. (ì.ki).(tà.pa). (ré.re).(pé.ha)		**!**** ** ****	** **** ******	

Chugach

In Chugach iambic feet are constructed persistently from left to right with one unparsed syllable in between. Stress falls on every syllable in position $3n$-1 (i.e. σ_2, σ_5 etc.) as well as on the final syllable of any words of length $3n$+1 (i.e. four, seven) syllables. Because of foot-persistence any pairs of syllables that are still left unparsed after directional foot assignment must be footed. This is unlike what we saw in Cayuvava. Consequently there is a local reranking in the constraint hierarchy with PARSE-σ coming to dominate over ALL-FT -L. Additionally undominated ALIGN-L tops the list of alignment constraints. The constraint ranking that predicts such a metrical pattern is

38. ALIGN-L, *LAPSE(DE) >> ALL-FT-R >> PARSE-σ >> ALL-FT-L

(38) is illustrated in the following tableaux for seven, six and five syllables. As before, the weak beats remaining unlicensed will be underlined.

39. Input: /maŋarsuqutaquni/Optimal output: (ma.ŋár).su.(qu.tà).(qu.nì)

/maŋarsuqutaquni/	ALIGN-L	*LAPSE (DE)	ALL-FT-R	PARSE -σ	ALL- FT-L
a. (ma.nár).su. qu.ta.qu.ni		*!**	*****	*****	
b. ma.(ŋar.sú).qu. (ta.qù).ni	*!		* ****	***	* ****
c. (ma.ŋár).su. (qu.tà).qu.ni			** *****	**!*	***
d. (ma.ŋár).su. (qu.tà).(qu.nì) ☞			** *****	*	*** ****
e. (ma.ŋár).(su.qù) ta.(qu.nì)			*** *****!	*	** *****
f. (ma.ŋár).(su.qù). (ta.qù).ni			* *** ****!*	*	** ****

In (39) the highest ranked of the alignment constraints is (undominated) ALIGN-L, which automatically determines that footing proceeds in the opposite direction of L i.e. towards *right.* Obviously, the *directional edge* of a foot capable of licensing a weak beat is also *right.* Any weak beat (or unparsed syllable) not standing close to the right edge of a foot lacks a licensor unless of course it is adjacent to a word-edge. For instance the three underlined syllables in (39a) do not abut either the right edge of a foot or any edge of the PrWd. This renders them defaulters in respect of *LAPSE(DE). Sub-optimality of (39b) is due to its initial underparsing of a syllable at the cost of undominated ALIGN-L. (39e-f) survive the undominated constraints but are ruled out for incurring non-minimal violations in respect of ALL-FT-R compared to the most harmonic (39d). (39c-d) are also passed by the undominated constraints and both score a tie in respect of ALL-FT-R. Evaluation thus passes onto the next constraint down the hierarchy PARSE-σ. The latter gives the verdict in favour of (39d) on simple parity count. Additional evidence in support of the principles of metrification under discussion is supplied by the following two tableaux for six and five syllables respectively.

40. Input: /akutartunirtuq/ Optimal output: (a.kú).tar.(tu.nír).tuq

/akutartunirtuq/	ALIGN-L	*LAPSE (DE)	ALL-FT-R	PARSE -σ	ALL- FT-L
a. (a.kú).tar.tu.nir. tuq		*!*	****	****	
b. (a.kú).(tar.tú). nir.tuq			** ****!	**	**
c. (a.kú).tar.(tu.nír). tuq ☞			* ****	**	***
d. (a.kú).tar.tu. (nir.túq)		*!	****	**	****
e. a.(ku.tár).tu. (nir.túq)	*!		***	**	* ****
f. (a.kú).(tar.tú). (nir.túq)			** ****!		** ****

41. Input: /ta.qa.ma.lu.ni/ Optimal output: (ta.qá).ma.(lu.ní)

/taqamaluni/	ALIGN-L	*LAPSE (DE)	ALL-FT- R	PARSE- σ	ALL- FT-L
a. (ta.qá).ma.lu.ni		*!	***	***	
b. ta.(qa.má).lu.ni	*!		**	***	*
c. (ta.qá).(ma.lú).ni			* ***!	*	**
d. (ta.qá).ma. (lu.ní) ☞			***	*	***

Conclusions

This paper successfully argues for discounting the foot-repulsion constraint *FTFT as a means of deriving ternary rhythm. But more importantly, it also justifies a reformulation of the anti-lapse constraint as *LAPSE(DE) instead of the existing one conveniently renamed as *LAPSE(E&K). In the restated lapse constraint domain edge i.e. directional foot-edge and word-edge function as licensors of weak beats in a grid. Foot dominance does no longer have any role as a licensor. The efficacy of this new rhythmic theory based on *LAPSE(DE) is illustrated first in explaining the ternary pattern of TB light sequences. It also proves its mettle in accounting for some cross-linguistic metrical facts namely the rhythmic ternarity noted in Cayuvava and Chughach type of languages.

Notes

1. This paper was originally presented at the International Conference on the Architecture of Grammar, 15-17 January 2002, at the Central Institute of English and Foreign Languages (presently English and Foreign Language University), Hyderabad under the title "Redefining *LAPSE" and was immensely benefited from interaction with the audience especially in terms of theoretical precision.

2. Hammond (1990) argues that Weak Local Parsing and extrametricality are functionally related: both produce parses in which binary feet are followed by a single unparsed syllable, either at the right edge of a word, or at the right edge of a foot. This is 'relativised extrametricality, that is relativised to a domain (foot or PrWd).

3. In his rule-based theory Hayes implements ternary rhythm by a foot parsing locality parameter whose two values as defined in Hayes (1995: 308) are: a) *Strong Local Parsing:* When a foot has been constructed, align the window for further parsing at the next unfooted syllable *(unmarked value of the parameter);* b) *Weak Local Parsing:* When a foot has been constructed, align the window for further parsing by skipping over a light syllable, where possible *(marked value of the parameter).* A binary rhythmic system selects the first while a ternary rhythm is the consequence of opting for the latter.

4. Ishii (1996) refers to the foot-based anti-lapse constraint as *LAPSE, whose formulation is identical to the PARSE-2 constraint proposed in Kager (1994). To avoid any confusion with regard to the grid-based constraint defined also as *LAPSE, Elenbaas and Kager (1999) in their paper refer to Ishii's parse-based constraint as PARSE-2. In the

present article there will not be much discussion of Ishii's antilapse constraint. But wherever necessary, we shall follow the instance of Elenbaas and Kager (1999) to refer to Ishii's anti-lapse constraint as PARSE-2.

5. Selkirk (1984: 52) proposes a Principle of Rhythmic Alternation, with an Anti-clash Provision and an Anti-Lapse Provision. This is cited below qua Elenbaas and Kager (1999: 281):

   a. *Anti-clash Provision*

   Every strong position on a metrical level *n* should be followed by at least one weak position on that level.

   b. *Anti-lapse Provision*

   Any weak position on a metrical level *n* may be preceded by at most one weak position on that level.

6. There should not be any confusion regarding the reversed relation between ALL-FT-L and PARSE-σ in the earlier constraint ranking for TB in (13) in §3.2.1 compared to the one presented here. This reversal is chiefly the fall-out of the use of two different constraints to account for ternarity in the respective rankings: *FTFT in (13) and *LAPSE in (19).

7. The mutual ranking between *LAPSE and PARSE-σ is immaterial in respect of production of non-ternary rhythms.

8. A strong beat, as a (prominent) syllable, is also a prosodic unit.

9. Assuming that each strong beat can license two weak beats — one on each side because of adjacency — and each word-edge can license two weak beats, theoretically, the total number of weak beats in a word (with one strong beat) would be six.

10. Considering foot-edge as a licensor of weak beats is not absolutely new. Hammond (1990) has already anticipated the idea in his concept of 'relativised extrametricality' according to which a single unparsed syllable can occur only at the right edge of a (binary) foot or at the right edge of a word. Ours however is a more generalized proposal in the sense that any edge of a foot can be the licensor of a weak beat depending on the directionality of footing decided by the relevant

constraint ranking. In addition, we adopt from E&K the view that every word-edge can license a weak beat.

11. These signal the directionality of footing with R standing for *right* edge and L for *left* edge. Data cited here are from Das (2001).

12. One can foresee a problem in a bidirectional system like Sentani with a word having a medial third foot distanced from the left- and right-aligned feet by two intervening unparsed syllables on both sides: (σ̀σ)σσ(σ̀σ)σσ(σ́σ). While *LAPSE (E&K) rules out such an overlong word, for *LAPSE (DE) this is perfectly 'grammatical'. However, in the overall constraint hierarchy there are other low ranked constraints, which see to it that such a form does not turn out optimal. For more details see Das (2001).

13. For greater details and typological implications of *LAPSE (DE) one is referred to Das (2001).

14. Persistent footing means any pairs of syllables that are still unparsed after directional foot assignment must be footed: (σ.'σ).σ.(σ.'σ).σ.σ → (σ.'σ).σ.(σ.'σ).(σ.'σ).

References

Das, Shyamal. 2001. Some aspects of the prosodic phonology of Tripura Bangla and Tripura Bangla English. Doctoral dissertation, Central Institute of English and Foreign Languages, Hyderabad. ROA 493.

Dresher, B. Elan and Aditi Lahiri. 1991. The Germanic foot: Metrical coherence in Old English. *Linguistic Inquiry* 22: 251-286.

Elenbaas, Nine. 1999. A unified account of binary and ternary stress: Consideration from Sentani and Finnish. Doctoral dissertation, Utrecht University.

Elenbaas, Nine and Rene Kager. 1999. Ternary rhythm and the lapse constraint. *Phonology* 16: 273-329.

Halle, Morris and Jean-Roger Vergnarud. 1987. *An Essay on Stress*. Cambridge, Mass.: MIT Press.

Hammond, Michael. 1990. Deriving ternarity. Manuscript, University of Arizona, Tucson.

Hayes, Bruce. 1995. *Metrical Stress Theory: Principles and Case Studies*. Chicago: University of Chicago Press.

Hewitt, Mark. 1992. Vertical maximization and metrical theory. Doctoral dissertation, Brandies University.

Ishii, Toru. 1996. An optimality theoretic approach to ternary stress systems. In B. Agbayani and N.Harada eds., *Proceedings of the South Western Optimality Theory Workshop (SWOT II). UCI Working Papers in Linguistics* 2: 95-111.

Kager, Rene. 1994. Ternary rhythm in alignment theory. Manuscript, Utrecht University. Available as ROA-35 from the Rutgers Optimality Archive.

Prince, Alan and Paul Smolensky. 1993. Optimality theory: constraint interaction in generative grammar. Manuscript, Rutgers University and University of Colorado, Boulder.

Rice, Curtis. 1992. Binarity and ternarity in metrical theory: Parametric extensions. Doctoral dissertation, University of Texas, Austin.

Selkirk, Elizabeth. 1984. *Phonology and Syntax: The Relation between Sound and Structure.* Cambridge, Mass.: MIT Press.

Vijver, Ruben van de. 1998. *The Iambic Issue: Iambs as a Result of Constraint Interaction.* HIL -dissertations 37. Leiden: Holland Institute of Generative Linguistics.

4

The 'Lazy' Speakers of Standard Bangla[1]

Introduction

Extensive researches carried out in the typology of word stress have shown that 'stress patterns are a domain of potentially conflicting forces such as rhythm, quantity sensitivity and edge-marking. Systems may or may not comply with all these three pressures, but the situation becomes intriguing when two cognate systems instantiate two different possibilities: one obeying and the other ignoring all or some of them. Let us take for instance the cases of two dialects of Bangla: Standard Colloquial Bangla (hence forth SCB) and Tripura Bangla (henceforth TB)[2]. In the former there is a strong rhythmicity requirement accompanied by quantity sensitivity. It also observes edge-marking although partially. By contrast its cognate TB does not yield to any of these pressures. Any theory of metrical phonology staking its claim on predictability as well as explanatory adequacy must be able to meet such a challenge with a unified theory of grammar as the two systems belong to the same language *viz* Bangla.

In the present paper we propose such a theory in terms of variable ranking of an almost identical set of constraints to account for the disparity prevailing in the two dialects of Bangla under study. Obviously our theoretical framework will be the Optimality Theory (henceforth

OT) as proposed by McCarthy and Prince (1993) and Prince and Smolensky (1993), and other subsequent illustrations of OT such as Kager (1994, 1995, 1999 etc).

SCB Data including foot types

i.

pa	'leg'	d̪oi	'curd'
gʰi	'rarefied butter'	d̪in	'day'

ii.

a. (´LL)		**b.** (´HL)	
[3]jú.t̪o	'shoe'	mál.ʃa	'an earthen pot'
né.t̪a	'leader'	céʃ.ʈa	'effort'
c. (´LH)		**d.** (´HH)	
ʃɔ́.maj	'society'	kut̪.ʃit̪	'ugly'
pú.ruʃ	'man'	ʃɔ́r.kar	'government'

iii.

a. (´LL)L		**b.** (´LL)(´H)	
pá.t̪a.ka	'flag'	pó.ri.mán	'quantity'
bá.t̪a.ʃa	'type of candy'	mó.no.jóg	'concentration'
c. (´HL)L		**d.** (´HL) (`H)	
ʃón.na.ʃi	'hermit'	bîʃ.pʰo.ròn	'blast'
prár.t̪ʰo.na	'prayer'	lóʈ.bɔ.hòr	'luggage'
e. L(´HL)		**f.** L(´HH)	
a.nón.d̪o	'joy'	po.rîʃ.kar	'clean'
gu.rút̪.t̪o	'importance'	ɔ.lóŋ.kar	'jewelry'

g. (´HH)L		**h.** (´HH) (H)	
ʃɔ́m.pot̪.t̪i	'wealth'	ʃɔ́ŋ.rɔk.kʰòn	'conservation'
ʃɔ́n.t̪uʃ.ʈo	'satisfied'	ɔ́n.t̪or.dhàn	'disappearance'
iv.			
a. (´LL)(`LL)		**b.** (´LL)L(`H)	
á.ra.dʰò.na	'prayer'	ó.bʰi.bʰa.bòk	'guardian'
á.lo.cò.na	'discussion'		
c. (´LL)(`HL)		**d.** (´LL)(`HH)	
ó.nu.kɔ̀m.pa	'compassion'	ó.bʰi.nɔ̀n.d̪on	'congratulations'
ɔ́.bo.t̪i`r.no	'descended'	pó.ri.bɔ̀r.t̪on	'change'
e. (´HL)(`LL)		**f.** (´HL)(`HL)	
ʃɔ́k.kʰɔ.mò.t̪a	'ability'	ʃɔ́n.ni.bìʃ.ʈʰo	'embedded'
g. L(´HL)L		**h.** (L(´HL)(`H)	
bi.ɽɔ́m.bo.na	'harassment'	ʃɔ.múc.ca.ròn	'co-articulation'
v.			
a. (´LL) (`LL)L		**b.** L(´HL)(`LL)	
ʃɔ́.ma.`lo.cɔ.na	'criticism'	ɔ.bɔ́r.no.nì.yo	'indescribable'
ɔ́.no.bɔ̀.ro.t̪o	'continuously'	ɔ.nút̪.t̪e.jì.t̪o	'unexcited'
c. (´HL)(`LL)L		**d.** (´LL)(`HL)L	
pɔ́r.ja.lò.co.na	'deliberation'	ɔ́.ʃo.mɔ̀r.t̪ʰi.t̪o	'unconfirmed'
		ɔ́.nu.bòr.t̪ì.t̪a	'obedience'
e. (´LL)L(`HL)		**f.** (´LL)L(`HH)	
ɔ́.nɔ.bo.cʰèd̪.d̪o	'inseparable'	ɔ́.nɔ.bo.lɔ̀m.bon	'remorselessness'
ɔ́.po.ri.hàr.jo	'inevitable'		

Stress distribution in SCB

Stress is distributed in the following way in SCB:

i. Disyllables: (σ́σ)

ii. Trisyllables: (σ́σ)σ, (σ́σ) (`H), σ(H´σ)

iii. Quadrisyllables: (σ́σ)(σ̀σ), (σ́σ) L (`H), σ(H´σ)σ, σ(H´σ) (`H)

iv. Pentasyllables: (σ́σ) (σ̀σ)σ, σ(H´σ) (σ́σ), (H´σ) (σ́σ)σ, (σσ) (´Hσ)σ, (σ́σ)σ(`Hσ), (σ́σ)σ(`HH)

Observations

The language builds foot from left to right. Foot construction is sensitive to syllable quantity. Length is not contrastive in Bangla. (Therefore a heavy syllable is a closed one.) The language permits iterative foot construction as is evident from a sequence of all light syllables. Quantity sensitivity either contributes to rhythm as final heavy syllables form a foot in odd numbered sequences or halts it occasionally at the prospect of formation of an (LH) foot. An (L) foot is disallowed in the language.

Problems

The following problems immediately emerge from the above distribution of stress in SCB.

a) The data show a dual possibility of foot construction: disyllables as well as bimoraic (considering that closed syllables initiate foot word-finally). But disyllables provide the crucial evidence that the former is preferred: (LH) foot though banned in longer sequences is allowed only in disyllables. Thus it seems justified to say that the language prefers bisyllabic feet overriding quantity sensitivity. Explaining monosyllables and final monosyllabic feet is therefore a challenge.

b) Although length is not contrastive in the language, a monosyllabic word and a final stranded heavy syllable in longer sequences always surface with a long vowel. For example, [g^hi:] 'rarefied butter', [d̪i:n] 'day', [pó.ri.mà:n] 'quantity', [ó.b^hi.b^ha.bò:k] 'guardian'.

Analysis

The problems above assure that rhythmicity is related to quantity sensitivity in the language. But they also demand investigation of the minimal word condition in SCB. Ghosh (1996) argues with evidence from vowel lengthening in closed monosyllables that codas are not moraic in SCB and establishes that the language has a bimoraic minimum. However, his analysis is restricted to monosyllables only as he does not include final closed syllable lengthening in longer sequences. Moreover, the shift of stress from initial light syllables to second heavy syllable and the presence of a secondary prominence on final (H) foot in longer sequences argue for codas being moraic in SCB. Again, assuming bimoraic word minimum, (LH) feet should have been permitted in longer sequences. But that is not the case.

For a unified account of the conflicting behaviours of feet in the language, we propose that foot is minimally bisyllabic. Monosyllabic expansion can be optimally explained assuming the presence of a virtual or catalectic syllable (Kager 1995) at the right edge of the proposed domain. Final stranded heavy syllables initiate a foot due to quantity sensitivity; but foot construction is accomplished by the word final catalectic syllable. Final light syllables in longer sequences, however, need not follow this phenomenon, as they are free from the pressure of quantity sensitivity of minimal word requirement. Catalexis also provides a unified account of vowel lengthening in closed monosyllables as well as word final stranded closed syllables in longer words: the coda gets linked to the virtual syllable thereby leaving behind an empty mora. For this mora to be phonetically realized, the vowel lengthens.

The problem that still persists is that disyllables prefer to build an (LH) foot rather than an L(H^σ) foot, defying quantity sensitivity (here 'σ' represents the virtual/catalectic syllable). We deal with this issue after having provided an OT account for the rest of the data.

OT account

Disyllables

In disyllables, stress is always initial disrespecting syllable quantity. Thus, disyllables of the type of (L´H) justify that it is preferable to build a foot on two syllables (disyllabic foot) rather than on a single heavy (bimoraic foot) which in terms of OT can be given as: FT-BIN is interpreted at the syllabic level. So there is a strong requirement on foot being minimally disyllabic in SCB, translated as the constraint given below.

(6) DISYLLABIC FOOT (DISYL-FT)

'Feet are binary under syllabic analysis.'

Another feature of SCB metrical pattern is that it constructs iterative trochees from left to right. This necessitates the invocation of the following constraint.

(7) TROCHEE (TRO)

'Within a foot, every '*' is followed by a '.''. (Vijver (1998:6)

The disyllabic trochee in SCB implies that the main stressed syllable of the foot can never occupy the final position in the prosodic word. This motivates the calling up of the following UG constraint for SCB.

(8) NON-FINALITY (NON-FIN)

'No prosodic head is final in PrWd'. (Kager 1999:165)

Another very strong requirement is that all grammatical words must have at least one stress. To capture this idea in the OT literature the following constraint is projected.

(9) Grammatical Word = Prosodic Word (GrWd=PrWd)

'A Grammatical word must be a prosodic word.'

(Kager 1999: 152)

All these four constraints are of equal rank and none dominates the others as is shown in (10) below.

(10) Input: /net̪a/ Optimal output: (né.t̪a)

/net̪a/	GrWd=PrWd	DISYL-FT	TRO	NON-FIN
a. (né.t̪a) ☞				
b. ne.(t̪á)		*!		*
c. ne.t̪a	*!			
d. (né.)t̪a		*!		
e. (ne.t̪á)			*!	*

Trisyllables

In SCB trisyllables, the primary prominence is mainly initial. However, if the second syllable is heavy (closed) and the first is light (open), primary prominence is shifted to the second. Also if the final syllable is left unparsed by the left foot, it has a degree of prominence if it is heavy. To capture this in terms of OT, the grammar needs to invoke the constraint WSP that regards quantity as sensitive to stress.

(11) WEIGHT-to-STRESS-PRINCIPLES (WSP)

'Heavy syllables are stressed.' (Kager 1999:155)

Notice that at the left edge in trisyllables we have three types of disyllabic feet (assuming feet are built on syllables):

(12) (LL) (pá.t̪a).ka 'flag'

(HL) (ʃón.na).ʃi 'hermit'

(HH) (ʃóm.pon).no 'completed'

Clearly WSP as stated in (11) is violated in a (HH) foot. Also examples like (ʃɔ́.maj) 'society' clearly argue for a disyllabic foot and violates WSP under domination from NON-FIN. The existence of foot types in (12) above therefore forces a reformation of WSP as done in (13).

(13) WSP (revised version)

i) Heavy syllables are prominent.

ii) A non-head $\leq$ head in foot.

However, both of the two consecutive heavy syllables are never prominent violating WSP (13i). This invokes another constraint that dominates WSP, formulated as the following.

(14) *CLASH

'No stressed syllables are adjacent.' (Kager 1999:165)

This is an undominated constraint in SCB. To justify the fact that primary stress is never farther than the second syllable in terms of OT, an alignment constraint that aligns the PrWd and the head foot to the left is proposed.

(15) ALIGN (Hd-Ft Left, PrWd Left) or (LEFTMOST)

'The head foot is leftmost in PrWd.' (Kager 1999:167)

Since primary stress shifts one syllable rightward under the influence of WSP, LEFTMOST becomes violable and is ranked lower to WSP. To capture the fact that a stranded heavy syllable must be parsed, the constraint PAR-SYL is also proposed.

(16) PARSE-SYLLABLE (PAR-SYL)

'Syllables are parsed by feet'. (Kager: 1999:153)

As a stranded light syllable remains unfooted either at the left edge or the right edge, PAR-SYL is a violable constraint in the language and is ranked below WSP.

The constraint ranking for SCB so far therefore stands like the following.

(17) GrWd=PrWd, DISYL-FT, TRO, NON-FIN, >> WSP >> LEFTMOST >> PAR-SYL

/anonḓo/	GrWd =PrWd	DISYL -FT	TRO	NON -FIN	WSP	LEFT-MOST	PAR-SYL
a. a.(nón.ḓo) ☞						*	*
b. (á.non).ḓo					*!		
c. a.(nón).ḓo		*!				*	**
d. (á.non).(ḓò)		*!			*		
e. a.nón.ɗo	*!						***
f. (a.nón).ḓo			*!				*

(19) Input: /poriʃkar/ Optimal output: po.(ríʃ.kar)

/poriʃkar/	GrWd =PrWd	DISYL-FT	TRO	NON -FIN	WSP	LEFT-MOST	PAR-SYL
a. po.(rîʃ.kar)☞					*	*	*
b. (pó.riʃ).kar					**!		*
c. (pó.riʃ).(kàr)		*!			*		
d. (pó.riʃ.kar)		*!	*		**		
e. po.riʃ.(kár)		*!	*		*	**	**
f. (po.rîʃ).kar			*!		*		*

Quadrisyllables

In four syllable words although there are fewer non-derived words than trisyllables, the above constraint hierarchy (17) holds good for both derived and underived words. The rhythmic pattern of alternating strong and weak syllables is distributed as secondary stress shifts from the third light to the final heavy syllable in accordance with the demands of WSP. The following tableaux illustrate this.

(20) Input: /alocona/ Optimal output: (á.lo).(cò.na)

/alocona/	GrWd =PrWd	DISYL-FT	TRO	NON-FIN	WSP	LEFT-MOST	PAR-SYL
a. (álo).(cò.na)☞							
b. (á.lo).co.na							**!

(21) Input: /onukɔmpa/ Optimal output: (ó.nu).(kɔ̀m.pa)

/onukɔmpa/	GrWd= PrWd	DISYL -FT	TRO	NON -FIN	WSP	LEFT-MOST	PAR-SYL
a. (ó.nu).(kɔ̀m.pa) ☞							
b. (ó.nu).(kɔ̀m).pa		*!					*
c. o.nu.(kɔ̀m.pa)						**!	

(22) Input: /abɔrjona/ Optimal output: a.(bɔ̀r.jo).na

/abɔrjona/	GrWd =PrWd	DISYL-FT	TRO	NON-FIN	WSP	LEFT-MOST	PAR-SYL
a. a.(bɔ̀r.jo).na ☞						*	**
b. (á.bɔr).(jò.na)					*!		
c. (á.bɔr).jo.na			*!				**

The constraint hierarchy proposed here so far comes to be challenged in SCB polysyllabic words with a final closed syllable. Let us, however, postpone the issue temporarily as the phenomenon is also noticed in monosyllabic words.

Pentasyllables

In pentasyllables also the secondary stress which is normally on every third syllable shifts to the fourth if it is heavy and the third is light. To capture the fact an unparsed syllable at the right edge is preferable to that at the left edge, the constraint that requires all feet to be at the left edge is also introduced at this point.

(23) ALL-FT-LEFT (ALL-FT-L)

'Every foot stands at the edge of the PrWd.'(Kager 1999:157)

This constraint however is the most violated one as syllables are required to be parsed into feet and there can be only one foot at the left edge. So the constraint hierarchy at the end of analyzing pentasyllables is as follows.

(24) GrWd= PrWd, DISYL-FT, TROCHEE, NON-FIN, >> WSP >> LEFTMOST >> PARSE-SYL >> ALL-FT-L

The following tableaux show how the final constraint hierarchy works for SCB words.

(25) Input: /ʃɔmalocɔna/ Optimal output: (ʃɔ́.ma).(lò.cɔ).na

/ʃɔmalo cɔna/	GrWd = PrWd	DISYL -FT	TRO	NON -FIN	WSP	LEFT -MOST	PAR- -SYL	ALL- FT-L
a. (ʃɔ́.ma).(lò.cɔ). na☞							*	**
b. (ʃɔ́.ma)								
lo.cɔ.na							**!*	
c. (ʃɔ́.ma)								
lo.(cɔ̀.na)							*	***!

(26) Input: /ɔbɔrnoniyo/ Optimal output: ɔ.(bɔ́r.no).(nî.yo)

/ɔbɔrno niyo/	GrWd =PrWd	DISYL -FT	TRO CHEE	NON-FIN	WSP	LEFT MOST	PAR--SYL	ALL-FT-L
a. ɔ. (bɔ́r.no). (nî.yo) ☞						*	*	***
b. (ɔ́.bɔr). (nò.ni).yo					*!		*	**
c. ɔ. (bɔ́r.no). ni.yo						*	**!*	*

(27) Input: /ɔporiharjo/ Optimal output: (ɔ́.po.)ri.(hàr.jo)

/ɔporih arjo/	GrWd =PrWd	DISYL -FT	TRO	NON-FIN	WSP	LEFT MOST	PAR-SYL	ALL-FT-L
a. (ɔ́.po).ri. (hàr.jo)☞							*	***
b. (ɔ́.po). (rî.har).jo					*!		*	**

Monosyllables

Monosyllables in SCB undergo phonetic lengthening irrespective of whether it is an open or a closed syllable. This phenomenon could have been explained by invoking the constraint FOOT-BINARITY (FT-BIN) which postulates that "Feet are binary at some level of analysis (μ, σ)" (Prince and Smolensky 1993:47). But such a possibility is precluded by the presence of disyllabic (LH) foot as against the L(H´) foot. But then how does a monosyllable fulfill the high ranked constraint DISYL-FT? To get round a similar problem Kager (1995) proposes the postulation of a virtual or catalectic syllable at the right edge of the prosodic domain. But the involvement of the catalectic syllable to build a disyllabic foot incurs a violation of the Correspondence (anti-insertion) constraint given below.

(28) DEP-σ-IO

'Output syllables have input correspondents.'

Although the phonetic correlates of catalexis is unspecified (cf. Kager 1995), lengthening may be considered as a consequence of a catalexis. Mora insertion or syllable insertion may lead to lengthening of a segment (syllable). Lengthening in a closed monosyllable in Bangla can also be accounted for as follows. The coda gets linked to the catalectic syllable. This leaves an empty mora (coda being moraic) in its place. To realize the mora vacated by the coda, the vowel lengthens in a closed monosyllable. As we shall see the same reason explains lengthening in final closed syllable in longer sequences as well. As an existing mora (here the moraic coda) cannot be deleted, an anti-deletion constraint is invoked.

(29) MAX-μ-IO

Input moras have output correspondents.

The violation of DEP-σ-IO in longer sequences occurs only to favor quantity sensitivity. That is only a final stranded closed syllable violates DEP-σ-IO and builds a foot involving the catalectic syllable. But a final stranded open syllable fails to do so as it is free from the pressure of quantity sensitivity (or even minimality requirement). So DEP-σ-IO is dominated by WSP and ranked lower than it. Logically, it is ranked along with LEFTMOST, as it does not interfere with initial (left) primary prominence.

The ranking order of MAX-μ-IO is difficult to determine, as it does not interact with any of the constraints proposed for SCB. Nevertheless, its status is that of an undominated one, as the underlying mora is not deleted in the language.

(30) GrWd= PrWd, DISYL-FT, TRO, NON-FIN, MAX-μ-IO >> WSP >> LEFTMOST >> DEP-σ-IO >> PAR-SYL >> ALL-FT-L

The following tableaux give the optimal candidates for the SCB monosyllables:

(31) Input: /gʰi/ Optimal output: (gʰi:ᵒ)[4]

/gʰi/	Gr Wd= PrWd	DISYL -FT	TRO	NON-FIN	MAX-μ-IO	WSP	LEFT MOST-	DEP-σ–IO	PAR--SYL	ALL-FT-L
a. (gʰ i:σ) ☞								*		
b. (gʰ i:)		*!	*							
c. (gʰi)		*!	*							

(32) Input: /d̪in/ Optimal output: (d̪i:n̆ᵒ)

/d̪in/	Gr Wd= PrWd	DISYL -FT	TRO	NON-FIN	MAX-μ-IO	WSP	LEFT MOST	DEP-σ-IO	PAR-SYL	ALL-FT-L
a. (d̪i: n̆) ☞								*		
b. (d̪in̆)					*!			*		
c. (d̪in)		*!		*						
d. (d̪i:n)		*!		*						

To extend this to longer sequences, final closed syllable lengthening is also the consequence of the presence of a catalectic syllable at the right edge of a word. For example,

(33) (pó.ri).(màn) → (pó.ri.)(mà:n) 'quantity'

(ɔ´.ma).no.(bîk) → (ɔ´.ma).no.(bî:k) 'inhuman'

We keep aside the undominated constraint GrWd= PrWd from the tableau for lack of space. But in the overall constraint hierarchy it continues to hold its position.

(34) Input: /poriman/ Optimal output: (pó.ri).(mà:n$^{\sigma}$)

/poriman/	DISYL-FT	TRO	NON-FIN	MAX-μ-IO	WSP	LEFTMOST	DEP-σ-IO	PAR-SYL	ALL-FT-L
a. (pó.ri) (mà:n$^{\sigma}$) ☞							*		**
b. (pó.ri. màn$^{\sigma}$)				*!			*		**
c. (pó.ri). (mà:n)	*!		*				*		
d. (pó.ri). man					*!			*	

The same constraint hierarchy also accounts for disyllables except that it fails to explain why a catalectic syllable is not involved to build a *L(Hσ) foot rather than a (LH) foot. This can be explained in terms of OT as follows. The two constraints DEP-σ-IO and LEFTMOST conjunctively (cf. Alderete 1995) make a constraint that is ranked higher than WSP but lower than the superordinate constraints. Therefore, the final constraint hierarchy for SCB words is given in (35).

(35) GrWd= PrWd, DISYL-FT, TRO, NON-FIN, MAX-μ-IO >> {DEP-σ-IO & LEFTMOST}>> WSP >> LEFTMOST, DEP-σ-IO >> PAR-SYL >> ALL-FT-L

(36) Input: /ʃɔmaj/ Optimal output: (ʃɔ́.maj)

/ʃɔ/ maj	GrWd= PrWd	DISYL -FT	TRO	NON -FIN	MAX -μ-IO	{DEP -σ-IO & LEFT-MOST}	WSP	LEFT MOST	DEP-σ-IO	PAR--SYL	ALL-FT-L
a. (ʃɔ́.maj) ☞							*				
b. ʃɔ.(máj)		*!		*				*		*	*
c. (ʃɔ́).maj		*!					*			*	
d. ʃɔ́.maj	*!									**	
e. ʃɔ.(má:j)σ						*!		*		*	*

(37) accounts for the final lengthening and ban on (LH) foot in polysyllables also.

(37) Input: /ob^{h}ib^{h}abok/ Optimal output: (ó.b^{h}i).b^{h}a.(bò:k^σ)

/ob^{h}ib^{h}abok/	GrWd =PrWd	DISYL -FT	TRO	NON -FIN	WSP	LEFT-MOST	PAR-SYL
a. (ó.b^{h}i).b^{h}a.(bò:k^σ) ☞							*
b. (ó.b^{h}i). (b^{h}à.bok)					*!		
c. (ó.b^{h}i). (b^{h}a.bòk)			*!				
d. (ó.b^{h}i). b^{h}a.(bòk)		*!	*				*

The crucial competition is between (37a) and (37d). The latter is ruled out as it violates the undominated constraint DISYL-FT that ensures disyllabic minimum for a foot in SCB. By contrast (37a) wins the fray as its final closed syllable undergoes vowel lengthening in addition to acquiring a catalectic syllable to satisfy the disyllabic minimum of an SCB foot. But is there any theoretical justification for such an explanation? Kager (1995) proposes the theory of presence of a virtual or catalectic syllable at the right edge of the prosodic domain. Thus a monosyllable fulfills the disyallbic word minimum as foot is built only with the help of the catalectic syllable at the right edge of the domain (cf. 31-32) above.

However, it seems that the speakers of SCB are not decided with the ranking order of the conjunctive constraint and occasionally a variation is observed where a L(Hσ) is allowed in disyllables too. For example /ba.l ĩʃ/ 'pillow', /nɔ.rén/ 'proper name' or /la.ʈái/ 'roller to fly kites' etc.

Constraint hierarchy for stress distribution in TB

Distribution of stress in TB

(38)		(39)	
pá	'leg'	p^{h}ú.ɖa	'hole'
d̪aó	'chopper'	pá.t̪il	'earthen pot'
pæ´k	'clay'	aít̪.na	'verandah'
t̪aîs	'haste'	t̪úl.par	'agitation'
(40)			
zí.ra.bi	'a kind of sweets'	ó.bi.ʃap	'curse'
pák.na.mi	'precocity'	ʃáŋ.ba.d̪ik	'reporter'
út̪.t̪in.nɔ	'passed'	ʃɔ´ŋ.rɔk.kɔn	'reservation'
(41)			
á.lo.sɔ.na	'discussion'	ɔ´.ma.nɔ.ʃik	'inhuman'
d̪úr.gɔ.ʈɔ.na	'accident'	pó.ri.bɔt̪.t̪ɔn	'change'
bî.zɔr.mi.ya	'bastard'	ʃáŋ.bi.d̪a.nik	'constitu-tional'
báp.zaiʈ.ʈa.mi	'adamancy'	ó.big.ga.pɔn	'intimation'
(42)		(43)	
ʃɔ´.ma.lo.sɔ.na	'criticism'	prɔ´.yo.zɔ.nì.yɔ.t̪a	'necessity'
ɔ´.ʃab.d̪a.nɔ.t̪a	carelessness	pá.rɔ.d̪oʃ.ʃì.kɔ.ta	'expertise'

Foot typology

From the above data we get the following distribution pattern for stress in TB words. Parentheses indicate foot boundary.[5]

(44)

i. (σ́)	iv. (σ́σ)σσ
ii. (σ́σ)	v. (σ́σ)σσσ
iii. (σ́σ)σ	vi. (σ́σ)σ(σ́σ)σ

There is no light versus heavy distinction among syllables in TB. The basic foot type is disyllabic trochee in words having more than one syllable. In monosyllables branching requirement of foot is fulfilled at moraic level. For a unified account, subscribing to the view of 'strictly binary foot' (Vijver 1998), we propose disyllabic/bimoraic trochee which is binary at all levels of interpretation.

Problems

At least two problems crop up from a study of the above data.

a) TB metrics allow only one prominence, which is inviolably initial up to penta-syllabic words. This non-alternating stress pattern is certainly a piece of counterevidence for any strong rhythmicity requirement. But one cannot designate the TB metrics as absolutely non-iterative either, since in hexa-syllabic words (the maximal of a non-compound word in TB) there emerges a secondary prominence on the third syllable after the main stress. It is important therefore to decide first if TB allows iterative scansion.

b) Assuming iterativity leads to the question of basic foot size of this dialect: is it binary or ternary?

Analysis

a) The strongest evidence for iterativity is the emergence of secondary prominence in the six syllable words. Explanation for the absence of it in tri-, quadri-, and pentasyllables crucially depends on the determination of the strength of rhythmicity requirement in TB and its basic foot shape.

b) Compared to SCB, rhythm in TB is obviously very weak. There is only one prominence –word initial – in words containing up to five syllables. The only instance of secondary prominence – in six syllable words – stands at a distance of two intervening syllables after the main stress.

c) Such a sparse distribution of stress at once makes one curious about the foot size of the language. Given the fact that words with three to five syllables have only one stressed syllable, initial, and that in six syllable words the placement of the secondary stress divides the prosodic word domain into two equal units of three syllables each, it seems justified to propose that TB has a ternary rhythm. But the proposition for ternary rhythm is seriously handicapped because of its failure to account for stress in mono-, and disyllabic words, which also share the same prominence pattern with three, four and five syllable words in having only one prominence, — initial. Suggestion of two catalectic syllables for monosyllabic words and one for disyllabic ones would be a wild one. But even if one takes such a stand, the theory fails to construct a second foot in quadri- and penta-syllabic words on the right edge because of the absence of any secondary stress. At this point one would feel provoked to think of the possibility of stressless feet. In fact there have been researches carried out along this line. Following Halle and Vergnaud (1987), and Hewitt (1992), Vijver (1998:36) feels it "useful to justify the existence of such phonetically stressless feet.....". Seeking to provide a principled account of the stress pattern in Modern Standard Arabic (henceforth MSA) Vijver (ibid) is of the view that "[i]t is possible to account for the distribution of main stress in MSA, if strictly bimoraic feet are assumed in which the head is only realized if it is also the head of the Prosodic Word, in other words, if it has main stress." The facts of TB however fail to comply with the MSA account as the former does instantiate non-primary stress which is phonetically realized e.g. in six syllabic words. Alternatively, to redeem the ternary rhythm approach for TB, the theory could be made to allow extrametricality of one and two syllables respectively in words with four and five syllables; and catalexis in one and two syllables in di- and monosyllables! This would certainly be a bizarre situation for any theory.

d) By contrast, a fairly convincing account of the TB metrics is possible if we assume binary trochaic rhythm with left-to-right scansion. Weak rhythmicity is then accounted for as a consequence of certain strong restrictions imposed by the language on optimal parse in particular 'feet should not be successive' and 'no foot should be constructed aligned with the right edge of the prosodic domain in other than di- and monosyllables'.

e) To set at rest the controversy regarding the (dis)advantages of ternary vs. binary rhythm in TB, the present paper argues that the necessity of ternary foot construction can be done away with if the grammar is constructed on the basis of constraint interaction within the tenets of OT. This is because to quote Kager (1999:142) "within phonology word stress patterns stand out as being typically governed by conflicting forces..." and OT is naturally equipped to capture interactions of conflicting forces." (ibid: 143) and resolve them through constraint ranking by way of producing the optimal form from a set of potential candidates. For one of the central assumptions of the theory is that constraints are ranked and violable.

OT account

To begin with let us first generate the word stress pattern in words of medium length i.e. those containing three-to-five syllables. We shall come to the extremes subsequently.

The major constraints proposed for SCB word stress pattern above hold good for TB facts too. These include GrWd=PrWd, FT-BIN and TROCHEE among the undominated ones and PAR-SYL among the dominated ones. LEFTMOST and NON-FIN however play variable roles in the two dialects. In addition, the grammar needs to invoke one fresh constraint to tackle the TB facts: *CLASH-FT. Compared to SCB, WSP and ALL-FT-L play no role in TB as in the latter syllable weight distinction is immaterial and rhythmicity is a weak requirement.

In the TB trisyllables only one foot is constructed on the leftmost edge of the word branching over the first two syllables and the final syllable is left unfooted. This is irrespective of the internal make-up of the syllables included in the prosodic words (cf. 40). So it seems that like the standard dialect, TB also imposes a disyllabic requirement on basic foot shape. This is, however, true only of words other than monosyllables. The latter throw up a serious challenge to the assumption of disyllabic word minimum by attesting surface vowel lengthening to meet minimality requirement. In brief, we observe conflicting manifestations of minimality requirement in TB: in monosyllables it is bimoraic while everywhere else it is disyllabic. To capture both the requirements in the most economical way we invoke the constraint FT-BIN, which uniquely subsumes both DISYL-FT and BIMORAIC-FOOT:

(45) FOOT BINARITY (FT-BIN)

'Feet are binary at some level of analysis (μ, σ).'
(Prince and Smolensky 1993: 47).

Since FT-BIN is an undominated constraint, no monosyllabic foot formation is permitted in trisyllables. Consequently, one syllable obligatorily remains unparsed in the optimal parse. By implication, therefore, PAR-SYL enjoys a very weak status and is often violated to ensure the emergence of the grammatical form. In the constraint hierarchy therefore it is ranked very low.

Before we go on to actually project the required constraint ranking for trisyllables a small but important technical clarification is necessitated regarding the interpretation of NON-FIN. The interpretation often accorded to this constraint is 'No prosodic head is final in the PrWd'. But in TB we notice that no foot at all, whether with primary or secondary stress, is allowed to be built on the rightmost edge in words having more than two syllables. To capture this fact we need to invoke the more specific version of the constraint as is stated in Kager (1999:151).

(46) NON-FINALITY (NON-FIN) (Specific version)

'No foot is final in PrWd'. Kager (1999:151)

Although not uniformly undominated as we shall see shortly in respect of mono- and disyllabic words this constraint enjoys a respectable status in the hierarchy.

Trisyllables

Let us now construct a mini grammar in terms of constraint ranking to account for the metrical pattern in TB trisyllabic words. As per the preceding discussion all the constraints other than PAR-SYL dominate over the latter and the former do not interact among themselves yielding therefore a hierarchical relation stated as below.

(47) GrWd=PrWd, FT-BIN, TRO, NON-FIN >> PAR-SYL

The following tableau tests out this OT ranking.

(48) Input: /zirabi/Optimal output: (zî.ra.)bi

/zirabi/	GrWd = PrWd	FT-BIN	TRO	NON -FIN	PAR-SYL
a. (zî.ra).bi ☞					*
b. zi.(rá.bi)				*!	
c. zi.(rá).bi		*!			**
d. zi.ra.bi	*!				***
e. (zî.ra.bi)		*!	*	*	

In (48) candidate (a) – the optimal one – wins out in the competition by virtue of its satisfying all the higher ranked constraints. Its single violation of the low ranked constraint PAR-SYL does not weaken its claim to be the most successful one since, all the remaining constraints in the fray incur at least one fatal violation of the undominated constraints in addition to sharing some violation each of PAR-SYL with the optimal one. A possible ternary foot expansion (48e) turns out suboptimal due to its multiple violation of the higher constraints. TB, by definition, does not make any quantity discrimination between syllables, which is why there is no theoretical mileage to be derived from an extension of the study into trisyllabic words with closed syllables (one or more). Accordingly, we now turn to four syllable words.

Quadrisyllables

In quadrisyllables there is a feasibility of multiple foot construction, whereas the language allows only one – initial. The undominated status of NON-FIN will no doubt provide the rescue hunch. But the lurking danger of a foot constructed word medially and flanked by one unmetrified syllable on each side needs to be properly tackled. To attack this issue, the grammar has to invoke the alignment constraint LEFTMOST which says 'The head foot is leftmost in PrWd.' (Kager 1999:167). This is obviously an undominated constraint in TB where the main stressed foot is always word initial. LEFTMOST therefore is ranked among the higher ranked constraint as we see in (49) below illustrated in (50).

(49) GrWd=PrWd, FT-BIN, TRO, NON-FIN LEFTMOST >> PAR-SYL

(50) Input: /alosɔna/ Optimal output: (á.lo).sɔ.na

/alosɔna/	GrWd =PrWd	FT -BIN	TRO	NON -FIN	LEFT MOST	PAR-SYL
a. (á.lo).sɔ.na ☞					**	
b. (á.lo).(sɔ̀.na)				*!		
c. a.(ló.sɔ).na					*!	**
d. a.lo.sɔ.na	*!					****
e. (á.lo.sɔ).na		*!	*			*

The optimal evaluation of (50a) over other candidates is self-explanatory. But the crucial point to be noted is that (50c) is ruled out as illicit thanks to the undominated status of the new constraint LEFTMOST whose violation the candidate incurs fatally. Once again it is of serious theoretical consequence to note that a ternary foot option presented in (50e) incurs fatal violation in respect of more than one undominated constraint and hence stands rejected by the grammar.

Pentasyllables

Developing an OT grammar for metrics is an interesting exercise in repetition with variation. Every bit of fresh challenge entails the introduction of a new constraint, which in turn triggers a chain of reactions in terms of revising the ranking relation amongst the entire set of constraints. In the following section we shall experience another round of such piecemeal grammar building activity. Let us now look at the metrical structure of the five syllable words in TB. As has been stated earlier this is the maximum length a TB word can have with non-iterative stress.

Addition of a syllable opens up at least one new possibility of metrification where two consecutive feet can be constructed without inviting any violation of any of the high ranked constraints — NON-FIN included. But this possibility is counterevidenced by the language. The grammar has now got the additional burden of circumventing such a potential candidate: (*´ *)(` * *)*. Obviously the answer lies in invoking the universal constraint against constructing feet in immediate succession namely *CLASH-FT.

(51) *CLASH-FT or *FT-FT.

'Feet must not be adjacent'. (Kager 1994).

Since in a TB five syllable word there is only one foot – initial, *CLASH-FT must be dominant in the constraint hierarchy. In other words the OT grammar for penta-syllabic words in TB will look like the one in (52) illustrated in (53).

(52) GrWd=PrWd, FT-BIN, TRO, NON-FIN, LEFTMOST, *CLASH-FT >> PAR-SYL

(53) Input: /ʃɔmalosɔna/ Optimal output: (ʃɔ´.ma).lo.sɔ.na

ʃɔmalosɔna	GrWd =PrWd	FT-BIN	TRO	NON-FIN	LEFT MOST	*CLASH -FT	PAR-SYL
a. (ʃɔ́.ma). lo.sɔ.na ☞							***
b. (ʃɔ́.ma). (lò.sɔ).na						*!	*
c. ʃɔ.(má.lo). sɔ.na					*!		***
d. (ʃɔ́.ma).lo. (sɔ̀.na)				*!			
e. ʃɔ.ma. lo.sɔ.na	*!						
f. (ʃɔ́.ma.lo). sɔ.na		*!	*				**

Emergence of (53a) as victorious in the fray is due to its non-violation of any of the higher ranked constraints. Three violation marks of the PAR-SYL attached to the optimal candidate is a faithful representation of the wellformedness condition on optimal parse in five syllable words requiring as many as three syllables to remain unmetrified fowlloing the initial i.e. left aligned trochaic foot. By contrast, the sub-optimal status of the candidates (53b), (53d) and (53e) is self-explanatory: all of them fail to satisfy at least one high-ranked constraint. (53b) turns illicit thanks to the crucial status of *CLASH-FT. Failure of (53f) owing to the violation of multiple undominated constraints once again vindicates our theoretical position that foot formation in TB, as in SCB, is invariably non-ternary.

Hexasyllables

So far we have dealt only with non-iterative foot construction in TB. The first and only instance of iterativity is attested in six-syllabic words where a secondary stress emerges on the third syllable after the initial main stress. There is however no motivation for constructing ternary feet. As we shall see before long, as in other polysyllabic words considered so, appropriate constraints and their right ranking are capable of accounting for such apparent ternary rhythm in terms of iterative binary feet. To accomplish this, the grammar, however, does not need any new constraint or any fresh organization of the ones already invoked and ranked. The tableau in (54) below justifies our claims.

(54) Input: /prɔyɔzoniyɔ̯ta/ Optimal output:
(prɔ́.yɔ).zo.(nî.yɔ).̯ta

/prɔyozɔ-niyɔ̯ta/	GrWd =PrWd	FT-BIN	TRO	NON-FIN	LEFT MOST	*CLASH -FT	PAR-SYL
a. (prɔ́.yɔ). zo.(nî.yɔ).̯ta ☞							**
b. (prɔ́.yɔ). (zò.ni).(yɔ̀.̯ta)				*!		**	
c. prɔ.(yɔ́.zo). ni.yɔ.̯ta					*!		****
d. (prɔ́.yɔ). (zò.ni).yɔ.̯ta						*!	**
e. (prɔ́.yɔ). zo.(nî.yɔ).̯ta					*!**		**
f. (prɔ́.yɔ.zo). (nì.yɔ.̯ta)		*!*	**	*		*	
g. (prɔ́.yɔ). zo.ni.yɔ.̯ta							***!*
h. prɔ.yɔ.zo. ni.yɔ.̯ta	*!						******

As is characteristic of OT grammar, emergence of the optimal form is calculated through a principle of minimal violability of ranked constraints. (54a), accordingly, incurs the least number of violations compared to any of its rivals and hence wins through. The marks of fatal violations attached to all other candidates, speak for the failure of their respective candidates in a keenly fought contest. However, a special note is to be taken of how (54g) turns out suboptimal. Compared to (54a), (54g) incurs a higher number of violation marks for PAR-SYL and hence loses the competition even though both of them fare identicallywith respect to all undominated constraints. This is an illustration of the OT provision that in spite of being the lowest ranked, a constraint can still be crucially active in the ultimate evaluation mechanism. Finally, one cannot afford to overlook the crucial evidence against the possibility of ternary scansion i.e. the suboptimal status of the candidate (54f). We have already seen such failures on the part of ternary expansions in other polysyllabic words. Yet (54f) has a special significance for the theory since it is primarily six syllable words that *prima facie* provide the major support in favor of ternary rhythm in TB. The suboptimal status of (54f) is a piece of clinching evidence to the contrary in addition to the others we have already come across in cases of three, four and five syllable words. Scope for further research however is wide open.[6]

Disyllables in TB

After having argued for foot binarity in TB mutlisyllabic words given the appropriate construction of the constraint hierarchy, it is now time to extend the scope of the same grammar to words lying at other extremes i.e. mono- and disyllabic ones.

To begin with, we shall consider the disyllabic words. One major point of difference that distinguishes disyllabic words from those we have considered so far is that in the latter no syllable remains unparsed, as the prosodic word is coextensive with a foot, which is a bimoraic/ disyllabic trochee. In other words, it seems PAR-SYL should be clubbed with the undominated constraints. But doing that will have serious implications for words of longer sequences as we have already seen in all of them some syllable remains unmetrified. The theory can still be rescued if we approach the problem from strictly prosodic point of view. Such consideration locates the problem not so much in the position held by PAR-SYL in the constraint hierarchy, but that held by the so far undominated constraint NON-FIN.This constraint was invoked to ensure that no foot is constructed aligned with the right most edge of the word in words having three or more syllables' length. This theoretical proposition now stands seriously challenged in disyllabic words where every prosodic word is minimally a foot – a strictly binary foot. As a theory of grammar OT however is aptly equipped to tackle such crises given its fundamental tenet that no constraint is sacrosanct: all constraints are violable under duress. This means the grammar needs a reorganization of the constraint hierarchy where NON-FIN will come to be overridden by FT-BIN, TROCHEE etc., but will continue to hold a position higher than PAR-SYL. The projected constraint hierarchy for disyllabic words appears as in (55) which is illustrated in a tabular form in (56).

(55) GrWd=PrWd, FT-BIN, TRO, LEFTMOST, *CLASH-FT >> NON-FIN >>PAR-SYL

(56) Input: /pʰuɖa/ Optimal output: (pʰú.ɖa)

/pʰuɖa/	GrWd =PrWd	FT-BIN	TRO	LEFT MOST	*CLASH -FT	NON -FIN	PAR-SYL
a. (pʰú.ɖa)☞						*	
b. (pʰú).ɖa		*!					*
c. (pʰú).(ɖá)		*!	*		*	*	
d. pʰu.ɖa	*!						**
e. (pʰu.ɖá)			*!			*	
f. pʰu.(ɖá)		*!	*	*			*

(55) is in fact a comprehensive picture of the constraint hierarchy appropriate for explaining the word-stress pattern in TB words starting with two syllable ones. One could however think of an alternative one exclusively specific for disyllabic words: i.e. minus the presence of

the low ranked constraint PAR-SYL. This is because in two syllable words what is of crucial significance is the dominated status of NON-FIN. But for a complete picture of the constraint hierarchy for TB metrical pattern PAR-SYL will always have to be restored to its due status.

Monosyllables in TB

Finally, let us look at the monosyllabic words. Monosyllabic words in TB are quite long on the surface irrespective of whether the syllable is an open or closed one. TB has neither vowel length distinction nor coda moracity. Consequently, monosyllabic long vowels can only be a surface or phonetic phenomenon. Again such phonetic lengthening is symptomatic of an underlying obligation on every monosyllabic word to observe minimum word length, which is equivalent to two moras. Consequently, formulation of a constraint like FT-BIMORACITY would have been a ready response. But such formulation of the required constraint will remain specific only for monosyllabic expansions. But the fact of the language is that monosyllabic words under affixation undergo proportionate reduction in the duration of the individual syllables so that disyllabic derivative stands temporally equal to that of the monosyllabic base. Formulating the constraint as mere FT-BIMORACITY will fail to capture this generalization ranging over both mono- and disyllabic words. To circumvent this problem, we have used the formulation of FT-BIN with the concept of strict binarity — whether at the syllabic or moraic level –subsumed under it. FT-BIN therefore is a crucial constraint for all types of word stress patterns in TB including monosyllabic and disyllabic words as well. There are of course other constraints like GrWd=PrWd and TROCHEE which join hands with FT-BIN to ensure the emergence of the minimum word in monosyllabic expansions.

But before we go to propose the relevant constraint hierarchy for monosyllabic words in TB, let us pause awhile and closely examine the issue of vowel lengthening specially in the light of its implication for the theory of grammar under construction. Vowel lengthening in monosyllabic words is a phenomenon both in open and closed syllables. In the latter, the role of coda consonant is negative.

To capture coda non-moracity in closed monosyllables an OT grammar needs to invoke a negative constraint that prohibits consonant moracity. (57) below takes care of this.

(57) *LINK-μ-to-[+cons]

'Consonants are not moraic.'

Obviously (57) remains undominated in the constraint ranking.

Codas being non-moraic, both open and closed syllables respond identically to the minimal word condidtion: both undergo phonetic lengthening under duress of minimal word and FT-BIN. Stated differently, all TB monosyllables undergo a mora augmentation to avoid subminimality. To incorporate this fact the grammar needs an additional constraint stated in (58).

(58) DEP-μ-IO

'Output moras have input correspondents.' Kager (1999:156)

As an anti-lengthening constraint (58) is very weak in TB: it must be dominated by the 'anti-degenerate-foot' constraint like FT-BIN (among others). In fact DEP- μ-IO occupies the lowest place in the overall constraint hierarchy since its violation is obligatory to ensure mora insertion in monosyllabic expansions. FT-BIN and *LINK-μ-to-[+cons] by contrast must occupy undominated positions. The constraint hierarchy for all types of words in TB therefore looks like the following.

(59) GrWd=PrWd, FT-BIN, TRO, LEFTMOST, *CLASH-FT, *LINK-μ-to-[+cons] >> NON-FIN >> PAR-SYL >> DEP-μ-IO

Let us test this out for TB monosyllables.

(60)	A. Input: ma	Optimal output: (má:)
	B. Input: d̮in	Optimal output: (d̮î:n)

A. /ma/	Gr Wd= PrWd	FT-BIN	TRO	LEFT MOST	*CLASH -FT	*LINK- μ- to- [+cons]	NON -FIN	PAR-SYL	DEP-μ-IO
a. F – σ – μ μ (má:) ☞							*		*
b. F – σ – μ (má)		*!	*				*		
B. /d̪in/									
a. F – σ – μ μ (d̪í: n) ☞							*		*
b. F – σ – μ μ (d̪ í n)						*!	*		
c. F – σ – μ (d̪ í n)		*!	*				*		

Candidate (a) in (60A) is the optimal parse for expansion of foot in open monosyllables.The important point to note is that (60Aa) shares the same number of violation –one—with the sub-optimal (60Ab) in respect of NON-FIN. But the former turns out victorious as it incurs no violation of high ranked constraint mainly FT-BIN. (60Ab) thus remains at best a degenerate foot with the properties of monosyllabic/ monomoraic foot, which is universally banned as a foot form. Same is the fate of (60Bc) as it renders itself subminimal by refusing to allow mora insertion. By contrast (60Ba) wins the competition by virtue of satisfying all the undominated constraints particularly FT-BIN and *LINK-μ-to-[+cons]. Violation of the latter constraints proves fatal for (60Bb) as it prefers to accord moraic status to the coda consonant against the facts of the language.

Comparison of the two dialects

A comparative analysis of the two dialects of Bangla – SCB and TB – reveals the following facts.

a) Both are trochaic systems with scansion proceeding from the left to the right.

b) Primary prominence is predominantly leftmost in both but in the standard variety it shifts, at the most, one syllable to the right under pressure of quantity sensitivity.

c) Rhythmicity is a relatively stronger requirement in the standard dialect.

d) Unlike in SCB, quantity sensitivity plays no role in TB. To account for these facts, in terms of an OT grammar, we propose certain constraints whose variable status in the hierarchy determines the natures of word-stress patterns in the two dialects. The undominated status of GrWd=PrWd, FT-BIN, DISYL-FT, and TROCHEE explains the identical foot shape of the two dialects: disyllabic/bimoraic trochee. The dominant status of LEFTMOST in TB is responsible for the invariable presence of the main stress foot on the left edge of the prosodic word. By and large this is also true of

SCB, but for the interference of WSP. The domination of LEFTMOST by WSP accounts for the shifting of the main stress from initial light to the second heavy syllable. In the non-standard dialect, weak rhythmicity is the consequence of the undominated status of *CLASH-FT and the high ranking of NON-FIN vis-à-vis the low status of PAR-SYL. By contrast, rhythmicity is a considerably strong requirement in SCB as ALL-FT-L and PAR-SYL hold important positions in the constraint hierarchy while *CLASH-FT is absent. Again, the main difference between the two systems evolves from the significance attached by each to the role of WSP, which is an OT constraint for quantity sensitivity. In the non-standard dialect, WSP plays no role whatsoever but in the standard one it has a significant bearing on prominence pattern.

As for the minimal word requirement both the dialects agree in imposing a bimoraic minimum. But in addition SCB also imposes a disyllabic requirement compelling the insertion of a syllable in monosyllables. In OT this is interpreted in terms of invocation of a dominated constraint DEP-σ-IO. In TB coda consonants being nonmoraic (forcing the grammar to invoke an inviolable constraint *LINK- μ-to-[+cons], minimality need is uniformly fulfilled by inserting a mora both in open and closed monosyllables and OT construes this as an obligatory violation of DEP-μ-IO in the constraint hierarchy.

Conclusion

In this paper we have accounted for the metrical patterns of the two dialects of Bangla, SCB and TB, in terms of OT constraints and their variable rankings. Both the dialects observe binary trochaic foot parsing from left-to-right. Dialectal variation however, expresses itself mainly in terms of the weak enforcement of rhythmicity requirement in the non-standard variety in comparison to the standard one. And this is accounted for in terms of the hierarchical reorganization of an almost identical set of constraints suitable for the respective systems.

Notes

1. This paper originally titled "Demotion of rhythmicity in two dialects of Bangla" is coauthored with Monoshri Mitra and was presented at the International Conference on Stress and Rhythm, Dec. 1-15, 2000, at CIEFL, Hyderabad. The paper benefited a lot from the suggestions of the audience present in the conference.

2. Standard Colloquial Bangla or SCB and Tripura Bangla or TB are two of the many dialects of Bangla. The former is spoken in and around Kolkata and is commonly known as *chalit bhasha* (i.e. colloquial language). It is regarded as the standard form of the language for both oral and written discourses in Bangladesh and in the Indian states of West Bengal, Tripura, and partially Assam. Tripura Bangla is a non-standard variety of Bangla and exists only in spoken form in Tripura. With its epicenter located in and around the state capital – Agartala, this is the commonly used non-official medium of communication for the non-tribal people of the entire state who otherwise represent one or the other of the following major dialects of the neighboring Bangladesh: Chattagram, Noakhali, Kumilla, Dhaka, Maymenshing and Sylhet. This is also the common means of interaction between the various tribes and non-tribes of the state. For details see Ghosh (1996) and Dhar (1977).

3. Whether the sound is an affricate or a stop is yet to be finalized. So the symbol /j/ is used here. Same is the case with c vs. tʃ as in cases like /céʃ.ʈa/

4. $^{\sigma}$represents a catalectic syllable.

5. This being the first formal approach to the metrical pattern of TB, the analysis here differs significantly from the one presented in Das (2001), and other subsequent studies. But this paper substantially contributes to a systematic study of TB metrics. Hence is its *raison d'etre*.

6. In fact in a subsequent study, the present researcher found it justified to revise the present stand as the ternary pattern emerged as a much stronger option for TB (cf. Das 2001).

References

Alderete, John. 1995. Faithfulness to prosodic heads. ROA-94.

Das, Shyamal. 2001. Some aspects of prosodic phonology of Tripura Bangla and Bangla English. Doctoral dissertation, Central Institute of English and Foreign Languages, Hyderabad. ROA 493.

Dhar, Prabhash Chandra. 1977. The segmental phonemes of Tripura Bengali and standard Indian English: a comparative study with pedagogical implications. M. Litt. Dissertation, Central Institute of English and Foreign Languages, Hyderabad.

Ghosh, Tanmoy. 1996. Some aspects of vowel phonology in Bangla and Bangla English. M. Phil. Dissertation, Central Institute of English and Foreign Languages, Hyderabad.

Hewitt, M. 1992. Vertical maximization and metrical theory. Doctoral dissertation, Brandies University, Waltham, Massachusetts.

Kager, Rene. 1994. Ternary rhythm in alignment theory. Manuscript, Utrecht University. ROA-35.

_____. 1995. Consequences of catalexis. In Harry van der Hulst and Jeroen van de Weijer eds., *Leiden in Last: HIL Phonology Papers*. The Hague: HIL Publications.

_____. 1999. *Optimality Theory*. Cambridge, UK: CUP.

McCarthy, John and Alan Prince. 1993. Prosodic Morphology 1: constraint Interaction and satisfaction. Manuscript, University of Massachusetts, Amherst and Rutgers University, New Brunswick.

Prince, Alan and Paul Smolensky. 1993. Optimality Theory: constraint interaction in generative grammar. Manuscript, Rutgers University, New Brunswick, and University of Colorado, Boulder.

Vijver, Ruben van de. 1998. *The Iambic Issue: Iambs as a result of constraint interaction*. Amsterdam: HIL.

B. Syntax

5

Bangla: A Language Without Subject and Object

A study in Pro-drop[1] phenomenon

1.0 Introduction

The LGB (Lectures on Government and Binding, Chomsky 1982) classification of Noun Phrases (or NP) is based on two features [± Anaphor] and [± Pronominal]. On the basis of these two features, each specified as either [+] or [-], there are four possible combinations. Out of these the one [+ Anaphor, + Pronominal] i.e. the overt counterpart of PRO, is ruled out for reasons which do not directly concern us here.

By applying the same typology for classification of non-overt NPs, we get once again, four possible combinations as is shown in the following table containing both overt and non-overt NPs.

1.

Type	Overt	Non-overt
[+A, -P]	Anaphor	NP-trace[2]
[-A, +P]	Pronoun	pro
[-A, -P]	R-expression	Wh-trace
[+A, +P]	——	PRO

Of these non-overt NPs, NP-trace and Wh-traces are derived through movements, PRO is base-generated. An NP-trace, like an anaphor is bound within its Governing Category (henceforth GC) by an antecedent from an Argument position as required by principle A of Binding Theory[3]. A Wh-trace is like an R-expression and in compliance with the Binding Principles C, it is free in the GC in the sense that it is bound by its antecedent in a non-Argument position (henceforth Ā- position). PRO is a base generated empty category which vacuously satisfies both Principle A and B by occurring in a position which is ungoverned and PRO fails to have any GC at all. Finally, coming to the non-overt corollary to the combination [-A, +P] the generative linguists have identified it as pro. It is subject to Principle B of Binding Theory (cf. Chomsky, 1982:78). pro is governed and its content is recoverable from syntactic clues provided in the sentence.

Italian provides good examples of such empty category. Let us consider the following sentences from Italian.

2. Gianni ha parlato
   'Gianni has spoken.'

3. e Ha parlato
   '*Has spoken.'

4. Gianni ha ditto [che [e ha parlato]]
   CP IP
   '*Gianni has said that has spoken'

In (2) *parlato* assigns its θ-role to Gianni. By analogy we assume that the same is true about (3) and (4) also. On the basis of the EPP[4] we postulate that there is a subject position namely [Spec. IP], in all the examples (2-4) above. The projected subject position of *ha parlato* in (3) is an NP position which is not phonetically realized and in which the external θ-role of the verb is realized. We assume therefore, that the [Spec. IP] position is occupied by a zero element. The zero element however cannot be a trace as it does not have an antecedent. Nor can it be a PRO because PRO must be ungoverned while the finite inflexion in (3) and (4) definitely govern *e*. The *e* in (3) however has a definite reference. Like a pronoun it may refer to an entity in the non-linguistic context or it may be co-indexed with an element in the linguistic context. In (4) one possible interpretation is that the non-overt subject of *ha parlato* is identical to that of the overt subject of *ha detto*. In brief, the non-overt subject in (3) and (4) is the missing non-overt NP i.e. the non-overt pronoun. It has the feature [-A, +P] and is represented by pro.

It is instructing to note that every language does not allow pro. A language like Italian (also Spanish) uses pro as the properties of this phonetically unrealized NP can be recovered from the rich agreement features. But as Huang (1984) has shown a language like Chinese or Japanese which entirely lacks in inflection also allows pro-drop. Borer (1980, 1983 and 1986) on the other hand has showed that Modern Hebrew makes only a limited application of the pro-drop phenomenon. Instead of going, therefore, into the details of this controversy as to what criteria exactly enable a language to drop pro our aim in the present paper would be to make a survey of the Standard Colloquial Bangla (or Bangla in brief) as it is spoken in and around Kolkata to examine if it observes the pro-drop phenomenon. For this purpose we take both Italian and English as standards to provide both comparative and contrastive illustrations.

The present discourse is devised as the following. In §2.0 I initiate the discussion on null-subjects in Bangla; §2.1 takes the discussion on to expletives in Bangla; §2.2 illustrates the instances of pro in embedded construction; §2.2.1 pro is considered as part of a chain; §3.0 provides more discussion on the null elements; §3.1 deals with the null-objects while in §3.2 the discussion focuses on the issue of control by the understood object. §3.2.1 extends the phenomenon to Bangla; and §3.2.2 gives us additional evidence of pro-drop from Bangla. In §3.2.3 I discuss the asymmetry between subject and object pro in Bangla. §3.2.4 deals with constraints on the interpretation of the non-overt objects while §3.2.5 highlights the issues in relation to interpretation of pro in Bangla. Finally, §4.0 summarizes the major points on Pro-drop parameter applicable across languages.

2.0 Null-Subject in Bangla

Any pronominal subject in Bangla as in Italian can remain unexpressed. But this is not allowed in English since English is not a null-subject language. Compare the following three pairs of sentences each from one of these languages.

(5) Italian

(a) io parlo.
'I speak'

(b) pro parlo.
'speak, 1.Pres.'[5]

(6) Bangla

(a) ami boli.
'I speak'

(b) pro boli.
'speak, 1.Sg. Pres.'

(7) English

(a) I speak.

(b) * pro speak.

The understood subject in (5b) and (6b) is syntactically represented by a non-overt pronominal pro. But in (7b) it is not allowed. Like Italian once again in Bangla also the second person and third person non-overt pronominals are recoverable from the verbal inflexions. Note the following illustrations from Bangla.

8. (a) tumi jao
'You go.'

(b) pro jao
'(you) go, 2 Pres.'

9. (a) Se jay
'He goes.'

(b) pro jay.
'(he) go(es), 3 Pres.'

But unlike Italian, Bangla agreement system does not make every feature specifications of the non-overt pronominal, with regard to person, number and gender (henceforth p-n-g), morphologically explicit. While only the 'person' feature is clearly indicated by the agreement system, gender and number remain indistinct in Bangla. Thus the pro in a sentence like (9b) above can be interpreted as any of the following in (10).

10.

pro = {
a. He
b. She
c. It
d. They (masculine)
e. They (feminine)
f. They (neuter)
g. They (combination of any two or more of the three genders masculine, feminine and neuter).

Inflection in Bangla therefore does not help one much with regard to specific information concerning gender and number features of the non-overt subject. These information are retrievable absolutely from the context.

2.1 Expletives[6] in Bangla

Expletives in Bangla as in Italian are realized as pro – a practice prohibited in English. Since expletives contribute nothing to the interpretation of a sentence, they will never be stressed and hence they may remain non-overt.

11. Italian

pro Sembra che Gianni sia ammalato

* seems that Gianni is ill

'(It) seems that Gianni is ill.'

12. Bangla

a. pro mone hocche joy ɔʃustho

*seems (lit. mind-in being) Joy (is) ill

'(It) seems (that) Joy is ill.'

12b. eTa mone hocche je joy ɔʃustho

It seems (lit. mind-in being) that Joy (is) ill.

'It seems that Joy is ill.'

It is worthwhile to note in this connection that while the typical expletive subject of weather verbs like 'rain', 'snow' is *it* in English and *pro* in Italian, in Bangla neither is used. Instead, the weather verb is replaced by a corresponding deverbal noun and is used as subject in combination with a very common verb *hO* 'to be' (cf. 13-15).

13. pro piove (Italian)

14. It rains. (English)

15. briSTi hocche (Bangla)

    rain be,3Pres. Prog.

    'It is raining/It rains.'

2.2 pro in embedded construction

To continue our survey of the behaviour and distribution of pro in lower clauses let us first look at the following sentences from Italian and Bangla.

16. $Gianni_i$ dice che [pro_i ha telefonato]

    Gianni says that has telephoned

    'Gianni says that (he) has telephoned.'

17. joY_i boleche [pro_i telephone korbe]

    Joy say, 3Perf. telephone do, 3 Fut.

    'Joy has said he will telephone.'

In both the sentences above — Italian in (16) and Bangla in (17) — pro is base generated with the features [-A, +P]. It is assigned the external θ-role of the embedded verb which is finite. Like an overt pronominal pro is free i.e. unbounded in its GC that is the lower clause. However, it is co-referential with the subject NP of the higher clause.

2.2.1 pro as part of a chain

pro can also be a part of a chain i.e. can be co-indexed with the trace *t* of a moved NP. To verify this statement let us look at the following sentences from Italian and Bangla once again.

18. Italian

[pro$_i$	e	stato	invitato t_i]
	is	been	invited

'(He/she) has been invited.'

19. Bangla

[pro$_i$	t_i	nimontrito	hoeche]
		invite PP	be, 3 Perf.

'(He/she) has been invited.'

Both in Italian as well as in Bangla and also in English the verb meaning 'to invite' is a transitive one and assigns both the external and internal θ-roles to NPs. With passivization the subject θ-role is absorbed and the object NP (here non-overt pro) is fronted (for whatever reasons is a different issue and should not detain us here). This much is common in all the three languages. But while English needs the Object NP to be obligatorily present in the syntactic structure, Italian and Bangla allow it to be dropped and one can retrieve the syntactic properties of the dropped NP i.e. pro from the AGR or agreement suffixes attached to the verbal stem. This is equally true of Bangla and Italian (allowing, however, for the limitations of Bangla with regard to gender and number that we have already noted earlier).

3.0 More on the null elements

To initiate further discussion on the null elements as a part of survey of pro-drop phenomenon on Bangla, let us ask the questions:

20a. How is pro licensed?

20b. How is its content recovered?

In answer to these questions Rizzi (1986) proposes that in pro-drop languages pro is subject two requirements:

21a. It is licensed under head government – in all the examples we have considered so far, the null element in the subject position is governed by INFL, a head.

21b. The content of pro is recovered through the rich agreement specifications.

As for the universal applicability of the (21b) of Rizzi's proposals, let us postpone the relevant discussion for the time being. Instead we explore the other implications of (21a).

3.1 Null-Objects

Head government does not restrict the licensor of a pro to inflection or INFL only. In principle other types of heads are also capable of licensing pro. This is in fact the case in Italian as well as in Bangla where the object of a verb can be left phonetically unrealized on the surface structure. These objects (or rather pro in object positions) are therefore, by analogy, referred to as null objects in these languages. Let us consider the following Italian sentences first.

22.

Questo	conduce	la	gente	a [PRO concludere	quanto	segue]
this	leads	the	people	to conclude	what	follows

'This leads the people to conclude what follows.'

23.

Questo	conduce —	a [PRO	concludere	quanto	segue]
this	leads	to	conclude	what	follows

'This leads (one) to conclude what follows.'

In (22) 'conduce' takes three arguments realized by the Subject NP 'questo', the Object NP 'la gente' and the nonfinite clausal complement 'a concludere quanto segue'. (22) is a structure with object control of the embedded PRO: the direct object of NP 'la gente' controls the PRO subject of the infinitival clause. In (23) the direct object NP is absent, but the sentence remains grammatical and again there is a PRO subject in the infinitival clause. This is rather puzzling: an object controller can not be omitted in sentences with obligatory control as in the following English examples.

24. This leads people [PRO to conclude what follows].

25. * This leads [PRO to conclude what follows].

3.2 Control by the understood Object

To account for the problem detailed in the previous section, let us consider the following sentences for Italian given in (Rizzi, 1986).

26.

L'ambizione	spesse	spinge — a [PRO commettere errori]	
the ambition	often	pushes	to make mistakes.

'Ambition often makes one make mistakes.'

27.

In	questi	casi,	di solito	Gianni	invita — a [PRO mangiare conlui]	
in	these	cases	usually	Gianni	invites	to eat with him

'In these cases, usually Gianni invites people for dinner.'

In the examples (26-27) the object controller is understood. In English the direct object controller can not be omitted, as can be seen from the glosses. An important feature of the interpretation of (23) and the example in (26-27) is that the implicit object is interpreted as 'one', 'people in general' etc. It has a nonspecific or arbitrary reading. Following the reasoning we have adopted so far in this paper, let us assume that in Italian the understood object is realized by a non-overt element, an empty category. Such a hypothesis allows us to maintain that the controller cannot be omitted in sentences with object control, thus accounting for the ungrammaticality of the English example (25) on the one hand and the grammaticality of (23), (26-27) which lack an overt controller on the other. In English, apparently the object cannot be realized as a non-overt category in examples like (25); in such cases there simply is no object at all. In the Italian cases like (23), there is a non-overt controller for the object, which can be presented as e as is done in (28) below.

28. Questo conduce e_i a [PRO_i concludere quanto segue]
    this leads to conclude what follows
    'This leads (one) to conclude what follows.'

3.2.1 Bangla

In the light of the above discussion let us look into the following Bangla data.

29a.

uccaSa manuSke [PRO bhul korte] udbuddho kOre
ambition man-Acc. mistake make to inspired do, 3Pres.
'Ambition inspired man to commit mistakes.'

29b.

uccaSa e_i [PRO_i bhul korte] udbuddho kOre
ambition mistake make-to inspired do,3 Pres.
'*Ambition inspires to make mistakes.'

30a.

durdin $manuSke_i$ [PRO_i porkrito bondhu cinte] Sekhay
bad time man-Acc. real friend know-to teach, 3 Pres.
'Bad time teaches man to know the real friend.'

30b.

durdin e_i [PRO_i prokrito bondhu cinte Sȩkhay
bad time real friend know-to teach, 3 Pres.
'*Bad time teaches to know the real friend.'

31a.

jOnmodine joY SadharOnoto SObaike [PRO nemontOnno kOre khete]

birth day-Loc. Joy usually all-Acc. eat-to invitation do, 3Pres.

'On his birthday Joy usually invites all to eat.'

31b.

jOnmodine joy SadharOnotoe$_i$ [PRO$_i$ khete] nemontOnno kOre

birth day-Loc. Joy usually eat-to invitation do, 3Pres.

'*On (his) birthday Joy usually invites to eat.'

In the three Bangla sentences (29a), (30a) and (31a) the matrix verb subcategorizes for an object *manuSke* in (29a) & (30a) and *Sobaike* in (31a); and a non-finite clause, with a PRO in the subject position. As co-indexation shows this PRO is controlled by the object of the matrix clause. But in (29b), (30b) and (31b) this object is dropped yet the sentences are grammatical. But the corresponding English sentences (as the glosses show) without the overt object are ruled out. The problem is exactly the same as the Italian ones in (23), (26) and (27), discussed in §3.1 and §3.2. Let us, therefore, justifiably conclude that there is a non-overt object in the Bangla examples (29b), (30b) and (31b) which is very much syntactically present in spite of the fact that it is phonetically unrealized. Otherwise the PRO in the embedded non-finite clauses will fail to be controlled rendering the sentences to be starred. Once again one θ-role of the matrix verb in each will remain unrealized. Let us therefore conclude that Bangla like Italian and unlike English also allows null-object or object pro-drop.

3.2.2 More evidence of pro-drop from Bangla

But perhaps more conclusive evidence as to the presence of object pro-drop phenomenon in Bangla can be gathered from the following sentences where the requirement of object control does not complicate the issue further.

32a.

puliS	pro_i	dhor-be	bhebe	[$corta_i$	palalo]
police		catch will	thinking thief		run Past.

'Thinking (that) the police will catch (him) the thief ran away.'

32b.

puliS	$take_i$	dhorbe	bhebe	[$corTa_i$	palalo]
police	him	catch will	thinking thief the		run 3 Past.

'Thinking that the police will catch him the thief ran away.'

33a.

baba	pro_i	marbe bhebe	[$cheleTa_i$ make joRie dhorlo]
father	beat will	thinking	boy the mother-Acc. embrace catch Past.

'Thinking that (his) father will beat (him) the boy embraced (his) mother.'

33b.

baba	$take_i$	marbe	bhebe	[$cheleTa_i$ make joRie dhorlo]
father	him	beat will	thinking the boy	mother Acc. embraced

'Thinking that (his) father will beat him the boy embraced (his) mother.

In (32a) and (33a) the object of the matrix verb is dropped. But (32b) and (33b) where these objects are overtly realized, show that these objects receive a definite θ-role from the verbs. Moreover, they are coindexed with the subject of the embedded clauses. All these lead us to conclude that the object is not really omitted in (32a) and (33b); but it is only phonetically not realized. Its syntactic properties and content can be recovered from the co-referenced R-expression in the embedded clause.

That Bangla allows pro-drop in the object position is further evidenced by the following simplex constructions in (34-35).

34a. [uccaSa maunSke mrittu-r dike Tene niYe jaY]
ambition man-Acc death-of towards pulling taking go
'Ambition leads (/pulls) man towards death.'

34b. [uccaSa pro mrittu-r dike Tene niYe jaY]
ambition death-of towards pulling taking go, 3Pres.
'Ambition leads (/pulls) (man/one) towards death.'

35a. bhalo gan Sarbodai manuSke anondo deY
good song always man-Acc. pleasure give, 3 Pres.
'Good song always gives pleasure to man.'

35b. bhalo gan Sarbodai pro anondo deY
good song always pleasure give, 3 Pres.
'Good song always gives pleasure (to man).'

The grammaticality of (34a) and (35a) on the one hand and of (34b) and (35b) on the other despite the minimal contrast that exist between them on the surface level, establish once again the fact that objects of these verbs *Tan* 'pull/lead' and *anondo deYa* 'to please/to give pleasure' can be non-overtly realized. They are not omitted. Because otherwise the θ-criterion of these verbs will be violated as is illustrated by the ungrammaticality of the corresponding English sentences without the overt objects in (34b) and (35b). Unless the objects are overtly realized the sentences will be ruled out. Remember, English is not a null-ojbect language. In brief Bangla unlike English allows pro-drop in the object position also.

All the examples on object pro-drop in Bangla that we considered so far, have one thing in common, namely, the implicit object is interpreted as 'one' or 'man' or 'people in general' —— all non-specific or arbitrary reading unless they are conidexed with a definite R-expression as in examples (32-33). This is a peculiarity which Bngla shares with Italian. We have touched upon this issue in § 3.2 and we shall take it up once again for detailed discussion in § 3.2.4.

3.2.3 Asymmetry between subject and object pro in Bangla

Now let us consider the following Bangla sentences where both null-subject and null-object are at work. But while the subject pro can be dropped both in the higher and lower clauses, the object pro needs to be phonetically realized in at least one of the clauses.

36.

pro$_i$ pro$_j$ hariYe felbo bhebe [pro$_i$ kOlomTa$_j$ bage raklam]

lose(ing) (throw)will thinkingpen the bag Loc. keep,1 Past.

'Thinking that (I) shall lose (the pen) (I) kept the pen inside the bag.'

37.

pro$_i$ kOlomTa$_j$ harie felbo bhebe [pro$_i$ t$_j$ bage raklam]

pen the lose(-ing) (throw-)will thinking bag Loc. keep,1 Past

'Thinking that (I) shall lose the pen, (I) kept (it) inside the bag.'

38.

* pro$_i$ pro$_j$ hariYe felbo bhebe [pro$_i$ pro$_j$ bage raklam]

lose(ing) (throw)will thinking bag Loc. keep,1 Past.

'Thinking that (I) shall lose (the pen) (I) kept (it) inside the bag.'

Both (36) and (37) are grammatical. In the former the object pro in the matrix clause is dropped but is realized overtly in the embedded clause and both are coindexed as j. In (37) the object in the matrix clause is overt but is phonetically empty in the embedded clause. Here in fact a movement is involved: the moved item is the object NP *kOlomTa* coindexed as j with its trace t in the embedded clause. By contrast (38) is starred because here the object is dropped in both the clauses. Notice that the subject pro is exempted from this requirement in all the examples (36-38).

To account for this we can perhaps take some clue from the inflexion of the verb. The subject pro is coindexed with the AGR in INFL and hence its syntactic properties are recoverable from the finite AGR. But the same can not be said of the object NP. The specific reading of the dropped object, therefore, is to be retrieved from its coindexation with an overt NP. Remember as we noticed earlier, in the absence of coindexation the object pro will get a non-specific arbitrary reading like 'man', 'people in general', 'one' etc. as in (34-35). In (38) the object pro fails to get even any such non-specific reading and hence requires an overt NP to be coreferenced with, which it does not get. This rules out (38).

3.2.4 Constraints on the Interpretation of the non-overt objects

Italian has a restriction on the interpretation of the object pro which should always be [+masculine, +plural]. The object pro on the other hand is always free. It is equivalent to the pronoun and depends on the finite inflection for interpretation. Let us consider the following sentences in Italian.

39.

La buona musica reconcilia e_i con se $stessi_i$

The good music reconciles with themselves (Masc. Pl)

'Good music reconciles one with oneself.'

40. un dottore serio visita e_i nud_i

a good doctor visits nude (Masc. Pl)

'A good doctor examines (his patients) nude.'

(39) contains a plural reflexive *se stessi*. Being an [+A] it should be bound within its GC to a coindexed antecedent, which certainly is not the subject NP *la buona musica* since it is feminine singular, while the anaphor is masculine plural. As the translation shows it is the

understood object e_i which binds the reflexive. (40) contains a masculine plural predicate AP *nud.* The plural AP again does not relate to the subject NP which is a masculine singular. Again the plural AP relates to the implicit object, which of necessity is [+masculine, +plural].

To account for these restrictions Hageman (1994) relates the issue to the general question of licensing and identification of pro. She postulates that subject pro is licensed because it is governed by the relevant licenser INFL and its feature content is recovered via the AGR features of the INFL which is rich in Italian. The head parameter implies that there can be licensers of pro other than the INFL. Rizzi (1986) proposes that 'the licensing of pro in object position can now be viewed as another instantiation of the licensing schema: in Italian V belongs to the licensers of pro, in English it does not.' (p. 519).

In addition, pro must be identified. Subject pro is identified by the AGR feature of INFL. For the identification of verb-governed pro Rizzi proposes that its content is established through a mechanism of *arb* assignment, which will associate arbitrary interpretation with pro:

41. Arb interpretation

Assign *arb* to the direct θ-role. Rizzi (1986: 521)

If *arb* in Italian is associated with the features [+masculine, +plural] then we expect that non-overt objects which are assigned *arb* should have these features.

3.2.5 Interpretation of pro in Bangla

There are two major implications for Bangla that can be derived from the above discussion regarding Italian pro interpretation.

a. In Bangla also subject pro is licensed under head parameter by INFL that governs it and the subject pro is identified by the AGR features of the INFL.

b. By applying the head parameter the object pro is licensed by the verb that governs and θ-marks it. As for the interpretation of the object pro one may find the mechanism of *arb assignment* quite useful provided one does not narrow it down further to any feature specification like [+masculine, +plural] etc. This is because as we have seen in the Bangla sentences, Bangla AGR does not make any specification for gender and number. We can conclude, therefore, that the *arb* in Bangla should be read as only third person with no reference to number or gender. Of course, this stipulation will be pertinent only when the object pro is not coindexed with any overt NP in the other clause as in (36-37). It is relevant perhaps, only in simplex sentences like (34b) and (35b).

4.0 Pro-drop parameter

In fine, let us take up for discussion the second requirement pro is subject to in a pro-drop language as proposed by Rizzi (ibid), repeated in (42) below from (21ii), where it was left unconsidered.

42. [T]he content of pro is recovered through the rich agreement specification.

As we have already observed, AGR is irrelevant so far as the interpretation of an object pro is concerned. But that a rich AGR is capable of recovering the content of a subject pro is also not attested across languages.

43. The pro-drop parameter

a. pro is governed by $X^{\circ}y$;

b. Let X be the licensing head of an occurrence of pro: then pro has the grammatical specification of the features on X considered with it.

Whether a language has any X° of type y licensing pro is a language specific property. Also the choices of X° varies cross linguistically. In English 'I' for example, is not the choice for X in (43a). Hence null-element cannot occur in subject position. In Italian and Spanish (also in Hindi) 'I' is a choice for X° in (43a). Bangla in this regard partially agrees with pro-drop parameter because both 'I/ we' can be the choice for X°, if not only 'I' or only 'we'.

Modern Hebrew poses a problem in that 'I' can be a choice for X° but only in a restricted way i.e. 'pro-drop is not allowed in the present tense at all and that in main clauses with the future and past tense it is restricted to first and second person' Borer (1986:392), Haegeman (1994). In certain cases the features of the governing head of pro will not be sufficient and hence the content of pro cannot be recovered. In fact this is the case in Bangla where the AGR does not pinpoint the number and gender properties of the subject pro.

Another problem for this account of pro-drop is languages like Japanese and Chinese which entirely lack in AGR yet allow pro drop (Huang 1984). Huang's proposal is, therefore, to argue that pro is possible in languages either with rich agreement or no agreement at all. This again runs into 'trouble'. Some languages, German and Scandinavian for example, as discussed by Platzack (1997) allow only expletive i.e. non-referential subjects to be non-overt. This could be related to the fact that INFL in these languages is richer than it is in English though poorer than in Italian. We could say that INFL may well license null subjects in these languages, but that AGR features do not enable one to identify a referential pro. The only option for a subject pro to survive in such a language would be when it is non-referential i.e. an expletive. By contrast, Bangla allows the subject pro-drop. But the AGR does not fully identify its features in terms of p-n-g; only p or person features are specified.

Taking all these cross linguistic evidence of either violation or partial fulfillment of pro drop parameter into consideration one would be tempted to think of a hierarchy of AGRs — from the least strong to the most strong — with the intriguing reservations that both the extremes resemble one another in terms of their ability to allow pro-drop. This suggestion may seem too simplistic but then the idea is perhaps worth pursuing. Bangla will then figure somewhere in the middle of the hierarchy.

Notes

1. The term pro-drop is used in Government and Binding Theory for a parameter which determines whether the subject of a clause can be

suppressed. Italian is a pro-drop language, because it can have subjectless sentences as opposed to English, which must have an overt subject. Other properties of pro-drop languages include a rich system of verb-agreement, free inversion of the subject and verb etc. pro-drop languages are alternatively known as null-subject languages.

2. There are at least four empty categories: PRO, pro, NP-trace or *t* and wh-trace *t*. PRO also called 'big-pro' is a term used in GB theory for a base-generated subject of certain infinitives. It can be controlled by some NP within a sentence, or have arbitrary reference: as in 'John tried PRO to please Mary.', where PRO refers to i.e. controlled by John; and again, 'It is easy PRO to please Mary.' where PRO refers to no fixed individual or referents (called R-expressions in GB). The 'little' pro on the other hand refers to a non-anaphoric null pronominal usually associated with subject position in a finite clause as in pro drop languages. It is identified through the morphological features present in the sentence as in Bangla sentence 'pro aSchi' meaning 'I am coming.'. The third type of empty categories refers to an NP trace or t as in 'John will be invited t.' where John actually originated as an object of 'invite' and moved to the subject position for passivization leaving behind a trace t. Thus John as an antecedent of t controls the latter. The fourth empty category is a wh-t where the wh-item controls the trace as in 'Where did you go t?' where the wh-word 'where' originates as the complement of the verb 'go' and moves to the sentence initial position, a formal need of English wh-interrogatives. the moved item leaves behind a trace t which is controlled by its thematic antecedent i.e. the wh-word.

3. In GB theory, the binding sub-theory refers to the module of grammar that regulates the referential properties of NPs. It captures the grammatical constraints on NPs and examines the relation between NPs in argument or A-positions. There are three principles of binding theory. Principle A: regulates the interpretation of elements which are referentially dependent such as reflexives, as in 'John hurt himself.' It imposes that the reflexives are linked to or bounded by an NP in an A-position within a certain binding domain. Principle B: Pronouns should not be linked to an NP in an A-position within the binding domain as in 'John hurt him.' where 'him' is not co-referential to 'John'. Principle C: Referential or R-expressions like 'John' etc are free in the binding domain as in 'He saw John.' where 'he' cannot be coreferentail to 'John' and vice versa.

4. In terms of LGB dispensation, sentence constituents are required for two reasons. First, for the minimal composition of a sentence an argument (i.e. an NP) and thematic structure (or theta grid) the predicate is a must. The sentence structure is thus determined by the properties of the words or lexical items. This property of a sentence is called Projection Principle. Second, expletives or semantically empty elements are required to fill the subject position in certain constructions since sentences must have subjects. This requirement is in addition to Projection Principle. In other words, lexical properties of words must be projected in the syntax, and in addition, all sentences must have subjects. The latter requirement is called Extended Projection Principle.

5. Number has no overt morphological realization in Bangla verbal inflection.

6. Expletives are what is traditionally known as dummy elements such as there, it etc. in the subject positions in English sentences.

References

Borer, H. 1980. Empty subjects and constraints on thematic relations. In J.T. Jensen (ed.), *Proceedings of the Tenth Annual Meeting of NELS Vol, 9*. Toronto: Department of Lignuistics, University of Toronto.

_____ 1983. *Parametric Syntax*. Dordrecht: Forris.

_____ 1986. 'I-subjects' in *Linguistic Inquiry*. 17: 375-416.

Chomsky, N. 1981. *Lecturers on Government and Binding*. Foris, Dordrecht.

Cook, V.J. 1988. *Chomsky's Universal Grammar*. Oxford. Blackwell.

Haegeman, L. 1994. *Introduction to Government and Binding*. Oxford, Blackwell.

Huang, J. 1983. A note on the binding theory. *Linguistic Inquiry*. 14: 554-561.

_____ 1984. On the distribution and reference of empty pronouns. *Linguistic Inquiry*. 15: 531-574.

Lasnik, H. and M. Saito 1984. On the nature of proper government. *Linguistic Inquiry*. 15:235-289.

Manzini, R. 1983. On control and control theory. *Linguistic Inquiry*. 14: 421-446.

Mohanan, K.P. 1985. Remarks on control and control theory. *Linguistic Inquiry*. 16: 637-648.

Platzack, C. 1987. The Scandinavian languages and the null-subject parameter. *Natural Language and Linguistic Theory*. 5: 377-402.

Radford, A. 1988. *Transformational Grammar*. Cambridge, CUP.

Reinhart, T. 1983. *Anaphora and Semantic Interpretation*. London, Croom Helm.

Rizzi, L. 1986a. Null objects in Italian and the theory of *pro*. *Linguistic Inquiry*. 17: 501-558.

_____ 1986b. On the status of subject clitics in Romance. In Jaeggli and Silva-Corvalan (eds.) *Studies in Romance Linguistics*: 391-419.

_____ 1986c. On chain formation. In H. Borer (ed.) *Syntax and Semantics*, vol. 19. *The Syntax of Pronominal Clitics*. New York, Academic Press.

C. Sociolinguistics

6

Standardization or the Politics of Marginalization: A Study in the Light of Freedom of Speech and Expression[1]

Introduction

Right to freedom of speech and expression is universally accepted in the civilized part of the world. In the Indian constitution this is enshrined as one of the fundamental rights accorded to the citizens of the Republic of India. This is also the essential premise of linguistic human rights world over. Article 19 of the Universal Declaration of Human Rights of the UNO states

> "Everyone has the right to freedom of opinion and expression; this right includes freedom to hold opinions without interference and to seek, receive and impart information and ideas through any media and regardless of frontiers."

So we observe International Mother Tongue Day globally every year. Language is an essential aspect of one's ethnic identity. But linguistic identity can also be coterminous with one's national identity. If linguistic, ethnic and national identities coincide, no trouble is anticipated but such occasions are very rare. More often than not, ethno-linguistic identity is at variance with one's national or state identity. And in such cases the interests of the linguistic minorities are the immediate casualties. Governments consider, in the main, the numerical predominance of the ethnic groups in according official recognition to a language. Denying official recognition to minor languages - an inevitable corollary of standardization - runs counter to the solemn proclamation cited above that in principle seeks to ensure freedom of speech and expression to every human being on this planet. Standardization of a particular language thus can easily be a handy official tool for the hegemonic agenda of those in power. Conversely, in the absence of any standard form, effective governance becomes impossibility. An ideal language planning must address this conflicting situation so that the issue of identity and identification, — more specifically, the issue of micro vs. macro linguistic interests— is resolved within the parameters of optimal democratic norms.

Standardization

Zeal for linguistic identity leads to the demand for protection and promotion of the one's language or the mother tongue. But what do we mean by mother tongue? Is it a language or a dialect? It is a sociolinguistic truism that language is an abstract notion while dialects are the reality. Every language is only a collection of dialects. But no language is represented by all the dialects, which belong to it; one dialect gets the primacy over the others and comes to represent the language as a whole. Thus emerges the standard dialect or the standard variety. It is worthwhile to consider the factors usually responsible for standardization.

By standard variety or dialect we mean the variety of language that has the *high status* in a community or nation and which is based on the *speech/writing of the educated, politically and socially powerful group. A standard variety is usually described in dictionaries, grammars, taught in school and universities, and used in media.* Certain factors and consequences can be culled from the above description of the standard variety:

a) It is associated with high status and hence becomes sign of prestige in a community or nation. The members of the non-standard varieties would feel an automatic urge to adopt the standard variety to overcome their sense of linguistic inferiority, which ironically is the result of standardization itself.

b) It is the language of communication used by the educated section of the society who also constitutes the politically and socially powerful group. Obviously, it is this group of the society who wants to establish and sustain their absolute control over the rest of the population. Consequently, their seemingly innocuous efforts at standardizing their own language and 'imposing' it on others are open to interpretation as a hegemonic activity in disguise.

c) It is the medium of instruction as well as of mass media. Society makes arrangements for its study as a subject in educational institutes. Students educated through this medium naturally would accept its dominant status without contemplating on any possible alternatives.

Critiquing Standardization

Creation of standard language as norm for educated usage is however also a necessity. Hence standardization has both merits and demerits. The relevant discussion is in order.

Merits of Standardization

Standardization brings into being Standard Language. Once a standard language has come into being it serves several purposes, which constitute the merits of standardization.

a) For the community i.e. social group, region or nation, state etc. it serves as a symbol of distinct, separate identity, as a token of independence.

b) Another positive outcome of standardization is that through it the community or nation-state gets a formalized, uniform linguistic identity that can open channels of communication between linguistically (dialectally) diverse groups and communities. This is important for people to travel across space, overcome dialectal differences, and get wider acceptability.

c) Again the presence of a standard language helps people forget or push below the surface their dialect differences and forge associations with one another. Standard language also facilitates smoother governance, wider communicability, easier and wider dissemination of knowledge, formal education and pedagogy etc.

d) Standardization enables writers, scientists, and thinkers to create newer repositories of ideas, thoughts and discoveries in the form of books, journals, and other forms of scholarly discourse.

Demerits of Standardization

Despite all these benefits standardization has some negative consequences too.

a) It acts as a powerful instrument for the domination of the elite over the masses. The Standard Language, because of its all-pervasive use in administration, bureaucracy, law, and various professions and most importantly in education, helps the elite consolidate and perpetuate their power.

b) Though theoretically the Standard Language and the benefits of standardization are available to all, in actual practice, the vast majority remains outside the sphere of the Standard Language. In turn, this vast majority loses out socio-economically and politically and is doomed to stay put in positions of powerlessness.

c) Very often these speakers of non-standard dialects develop strong negative perceptions of their own varieties and even of their own speech communities.

These negative perceptions over a period of time get fixed in their psyche and become obstacles in their full participation in national/

regional enterprise. In other words, distinction for one dialect or language implies discrimination against others. This brings us to the issue of linguistic marginalization or the emergence of the "Other".

Emergence of the "Other"

One of the consequences of standardization of a particular dialect belonging to one language, is the emergence of the term "non-standard' to designate the rest of the dialects of the same language. Stated differently, if the standard variety provides the NORM, the non-standard ones get clubbed, by implication, under the umbrella term the "OTHER". In course of time, these "Others" are subjected to the same process of marginalization that we notice in any other sphere of life where a binary method of opposition not only reorganizes the facts of the phenomenal world but also snugly introduces hierarchization. So Man is the NORM or STANDARD who represents humanity in general while Woman is "OTHER" to Man". Again, Gold is the NORM and rest of the metals constitutes the "OTHER" to it. In this way, an oppositional hierarchy defines the categories of human experiences according to NORM vs. OTHER. But the story does not end here. Nor is it so simple.

This apparently harmless distinction can have long-lasting and even ineradicable sociopolitical effects. In terms of color distinction, for instance, White is regarded as the NORM while the rest are "OTHERS" to it. That means, any color other than "White", the color of the White people, is inferior, ugly and hence hateful; those who possess these "OTHERS" are therefore, 'barbaric', 'uncivilized', and 'need be civilized' and 'can be rightfully exploited' in the name of civilizing them. The result is apartheid, colonization and racism. The list can be prolonged to include class-discrimination, caste-discrimination, sex-based discrimination, education based discrimination, and language based discrimination and many others that we come across in all most every sphere of our life.

Rise of new standards

Linguistic "Otherness", the direct fallout of standardization, is inseparably linked with the issue of identity especially of the minority. These marginal groups in the absence of any official recognition of their languages feel themselves isolated from the mainstream. They feel their ethno-cultural identity threatened; and develop a psychological blockade towards the mainstream activities of the state and nation. In course of time their quest for identity compels them to create alternative centers of identity, an attempt that in political terms is dabbed as separatism, regionalism, secessionism etc. etc. The ratio of the growth of such centers is proportionate to the degree of official indifference to the identity quest of the marginalized.

No government, however, can afford to give recognition to all these new and parallel centers of identity who seek to throw up new standards, if not totally redefine the existing one. They want to create separate nation, state, autonomous territory etc. etc. where they think their ethno-linguistic identity would be duly safeguarded. Hence we observed the emergence of many Indian states demarcated on the basis of ethno-linguistic homogeneity. Linguistic conflicts due to divided ethnic and national loyalties are often bitter and violent. In recent years, there have been major incidents in several countries such as India, Spain, Canada, Belgium, Corsica, the USA, South Africa, and the Celtic speaking areas. The reasons for conflict vary greatly:

a) In some cases, the use of a language is declining, and the reaction is a desperate attempt to keep it, and the community it represents, alive;

b) In others, a minority group may be rapidly growing in numbers, so that its language begins to compete with the established languages of the country for educational, media, and other sources;

c) In still other cases the number of speakers may be stable, but there has been an awakening or reawakening of cultural identity, with a subsequent demand for recognition and usually territorial independence.

Suggestion for Reconciliation

Any number of suggestions can be offered to get rid of such a situation of conflicting identities involving language. Such suggestions range from the most undemocratic and autocratic one of imposing the language of the dominant sections, i.e. the standard language, on the linguistic minorities as an obligatory means for all official and other formal communications. This was the case when Urdu was sought to be imposed by force on the people of the then East Pakistan (Now Bangladesh) whose mother tongue is predominantly Bangla i.e. the various dialects of Bangla. The result was a bloody resistance by the latter and the subsequent secession of Eastern part of Pakistan and the emergence of Bangladesh in the long run. At the other extreme would be a total surrender of the national government of the country to these ever-increasing pressures and the acceptance of all the new standards as signs of ethno-linguistic identity of the marginalized linguistic groups. No doubt, in such a situation, the country's national integrity and political sovereignty would be the immediate casualty.

Neither of the solutions as such sounds practicable: in the first case there would be total tyranny and violation of human rights while in case of the latter it will be a state of absolute anarchy with so many parallel centers of power.

A more democratic mean could however be suggested and it is as follows. In terms of the insights of the generative linguistics all linguistic diversities are only surface phenomena while underlyingly there exists a deep-rooted uniformity. This is proved by language typology as well as child language acquisition facts. Differences between cognate dialects and languages are easily predictable and confined mainly to phonological and morphological variations. Even allowing for the role, played by emotion and sentiment in matters of ethno-linguistic identity, such information if carefully disseminated among the warring groups could go a long way in pacifying the heat generated by the sense of mutual distrust and deprivation. Along with this, and this is more practicable and rational, arrangements could be made by the textbook producers, media personnel, and language planners in general to make room for the accommodation of the linguistic items from the non-standard varieties into the standard one. This inclusiveness of attitude would not only lend the standard version a more generalized and democratic flavor, but also make the marginalized sections i.e. the linguistic minorities feel more friendly and comfortable vis-à-vis the standard language. The psychological bond between the Standard and the "Others" would thus be stronger and more lasting. In fact, this would be a kind of planned borrowing aimed at ensuring greater participation by all sections of the population, despite linguistic and dialectal differences. All living languages enrich themselves through borrowing from other sources. If borrowing from the "Other" languages and dialects helps the cause of ethno-linguistic as well a national integration, borrowing is certainly a welcome move.

Conclusion

This paper, without being particular to any specific tribal or other language situation, addresses the issue of linguistic identity of the minorities, and their identification with the predominant variety and group, in a multilingual situation. The conflict between the two is the result of quest for ethno-linguistic identity by all homogeneous speech communities as opposed to the compulsion to accept the standard variety as an obligatory means for at least all formal communications. Since, in the light of our past experience, no lasting solution can be visualized in terms of Hobson's choice, a golden mean is the need of the hour. Such an optimum situation could be ensured only if the idea of the underlying uniformity of all human languages despite their surface diversity is made a part of the common knowledge of the warring linguistic groups; and if the standard language becomes more accommodative towards the linguistic diversity of those who constitute the linguistic "OTHER".

Note

1. This paper was originally presented at the ICHR National Seminar on "The Tribes, Peasants and Modern Identity in the North Eastern India c.1800-2000 A. D." April 5-7, 2006.

References

Chambers, I. K. and Peter Trudgill. 1998. *Dialectology.* UK. CUP.

Crystal, David. 1997. *The Cambridge Encyclopedia of Language. Cambridge.* UK. CUP.

McArthur, Tom. 1992. *The Oxford Companion to the English Language.* Oxford, New York. OUP.

Rajawat, Mamta. 2001. *Burning Issues of Human Rights.* New Delhi. Kalpaz Publications.

Spivak, Gayatri Chakraborty. 1987. "Mahasweta Devi's 'Stanadayini'". *In Subaltern Studies v.: Writings on South Asian History and Society,* Ranajit Guha (eds.). New Delhi, OUP.

Sturrock, John. 1986/2003. *Structuralism.* USA. Blackwell.

7

Is De-centering for De-centering Well-centered?[1]

Introduction

The small state of the Indian federation called Tripura, like most of the remaining North East Indian states, has of late made its mark in the national and international scenario though for a 'wrong' cause. Since the late 70s it has made itself notorious, despite its economic, educational and socio-political achievements, for its ethnic unrest leading to large-scale violence and subsequent polarization along the line of ethnic divide. Narrow political interest no doubt played its part in fumigating an atmosphere of mutual distrust between the two broad ethno-linguistic communities - the majority Bengalis and the minority tribesmen. While the former are mostly immigrants from across the border, which came into existence following the partition of India as one of the crucial conditions of Independence, the latter, belonging primarily to the various Mongoloid tribes of Asia, are allegedly the 'sons of the soil'. Once the immigrants gained in power and economy, not always through fair means though, and started asserting themselves, it gave rise to an antithetical awareness of self-control and self-identity among the tribes of the state. A polarization followed resulting in a sentiment of jingoism especially among the ethnic minority. The sporadic incidences of terrorist violence often accompanied by ethnic tension are reminders of the dark days of the 1980s. In recent times however, this ethno-linguistic tussle has taken a rather 'democratic' turn with the minority tribes trying to counter-assert themselves through their demands for a separate linguistic identity. On the surface, there is nothing harmful in it since right to the freedom of speech and, hence of language is universally recognized. The UN declaration on linguistic human rights and the fundamental right of freedom of speech enshrined in the Constitution of India are some examples in order. But on a closer analysis, the demand for linguistic identity turns out to be a subtle attempt at linguistic homogenization by the major tribes. This is followed by the issue of *selecting* the medium for orthographic representation of the tribal 'lingua franca' namely Kokbarak. The tribal intelligentsia is divided on this issue i.e. what should be the script for written Kokbarak — Bengali script or roman script.

In this paper, I would argue that both the demands are in fact interrelated in the sense that one takes the cue from the other. Both can be interpreted as a quest for distinct self-identity far away from the hegemony of the center. In this sense both are consequences of the urge for de-centering. But while the former illustrates qualified accordance to de-centering, the other illustrates the unhealthy consequences of de-centering resulting in a collective vertigo. I wind up the discussion, arguing for a qualified de-centering based on pragmatic considerations and against any mad frenzy of 'decentering for de-centering' jeopardizing man's fundamental identity as a social being.

Standardizing language

Zeal for linguistic identity leads to the demand for protection and promotion of one's language or the mother tongue. But what do we mean by mother tongue? Is it a language or a dialect? It is a sociolinguistic truism that language is an abstract notion while dialects are the reality. Every language is only a collection of dialects. But no language is represented by all the dialects, which belong to it; one dialect gets the primacy over the others and comes to represent the language as a whole. Thus emerges the standard dialect or the standard variety. It is worthwhile to consider the factors usually responsible for standardization.

By standard variety or dialect we mean the variety of language that has the *high status* in a community or nation and which is based on the *speech/writing of the educated, politically and socially powerful group. A standard variety is usually described in dictionaries, grammars, taught in school and universities, and used in media.* Certain factors and consequences can be culled from the above description of the standard variety:

a) It is associated with high status and hence becomes sign of prestige in a community or nation. The members of the non-standard varieties would feel an automatic urge to adopt the standard variety to overcome their sense of linguistic inferiority, which ironically is the result of standardization itself.

b) It is the language of communication used by the educated section of the society who also constitutes the politically and socially powerful group. Obviously, it is this group of the society who wants to establish and sustain their control over the rest of the population. Consequently, their seemingly innocuous efforts at standardizing their own language and 'imposing' it on others are open to interpretation as a hegemonic activity in disguise.

c) It is the medium of instruction as well as of mass media. Society makes arrangements for its study as a subject in educational institutes. Students educated through this medium naturally would accept its dominant status without contemplating on any possible alternatives.

Standardization of Kokbarak: a fulfillment of the demand for identity

In Tripura there are as many as nineteen tribes which include the Debbarmas, Tripuras, Jamatias, Reangs, Murashings, Noatias, Kolois, Rupinis, Uchois, Darlongs, Kukis, Khashis, Oraons, Santals, Munda,

Lusais, Mogs, Chakmas, and Halams. Of these the first nine constitute the majority and speak Kokbarak. The latter is therefore recognized by the authority as the representative of the tribal languages in Tripura. So far, so good. But in the process of standardizing Kokbarak, the languages of the remaining tribes, albeit minority gets 'derecognized' so to say, as far as the official stand is concerned. They either feel the pressure to switch over to the standardized variety at the cost of their own or get alienated from the main stream of social and political life. A third possibility is that they turn violent to assert their independent identity and thereby create pressure on those in power to pay due attention to their cause. In consequence of the third option, they earn the pejorative appellations like secessionists, separatists, extremists, jingoists etc. etc. The irony of the fact is that it is the same process of struggles through which the major tribes got recognition for their language/s or dialects. So the entire issue boils down to the cliché that numerical majority and soico-economic as well as political clout is the most important precondition for getting one's ethno-linguistic identity recognized. Lacking this, one's ethno-linguistic identity either has to be sacrificed to the hegemonic agenda of the major tribes or "turn violently vocal in defence of one's ethno-linguistic identity inviting oppressive measures from the authority or center. This runs counter to the Universal Declaration of Human Rights of the UNO which states

> "Everyone has the right to freedom of opinion and expression; this right includes freedom to hold opinions without interference and to seek, receive and impart information and ideas through any media and regardless of frontiers."

Standardization of a particular language thus can easily be a handy official tool for the hegemonic agenda of those in power and result in a planned denial of privileges to those who belong to the linguistic minority. In course of time this newly defined marginalized sections form a fresh pressure group and the process is never-ending.

Script debate

The now-famous debate over deciding the script for Kokbarak

can not be seen in isolation from the above-discussed process of emergence of fresh pressure groups in the name of recognition for ethno-linguistic identity. The presumably same people who once fought unitedly for achieving the goal of getting their language, namely Kokbarak, recognized as a mark of their ethnic and cultural identity, are now divided over the issue of script for Kokbarak. A look into the background to the emergence of such split interest would be extremely relevant at this point and for this part of the discussion I am indebted to Chaudhury (2006).

Bengali script

According to the researcher, it is established through glottochronology that Kokbarak had emerged from Dimasa, a language of the Bodo-Naga branch of the Tibeto-Burmese language family in between 12th to 14th centuries. For its written form, the Kokbarak speakers found the Bengali script available within their reach. Hence it was natural that Kokbark orthography first appeared in Bengali script in between thirteenth and fourteenth centuries. Historically, the Mongoloid kings of Tipperah ruled over a vast piece of plain land now belonging to the adjacent districts of Bangladesh. Their subjects were mostly Bengalis whose script and language therefore were easily available to the Kokborak speakers. Thereafter, many people contributed to the wider use of Bengali script for Kokbarak orthography. Most notable among them was the biography of King Mahendra Manikya by Duragaprasad Narayan in 1703. This is regarded as the first extant record of written Kokbarak. In the second phase, we see the contributions of Radha Mohan Thakur, Kazi Daulat Ahmed etc. to Kokbarak literature. Later on writers like Sudhanna Debbarma, Dasharath Debbarma, Mahendra Debbarma, Ajitbandhu Debbarma, Banshi Thakur, Adviser Jiten Thakur - all activists of the Jana Shiksha Movement — made substantial contributions to the enrichment of Kokbarak language and literature. At present a large number of creative writers is busy in enhancing Kokbarak literature to a national and international acclaim. In 1967 there was formed Kokbarak Unnayan Porishad which invited Dr. Suhash Chaudhury, a Chicago University trained linguist for conducting a scientific study of Kokbarak language and suggesting an alphabet to capture its speech sounds, among other objectives. After having made a comparative analysis Dr. Chatterjee arrived at a conclusion that scientifically both Bengali and Roman scripts could be the right alphabet for Kokbarak. However, for pragmatic reasons he gave the verdict in favour of Bengali script since the latter was easily available and already familiar to the Kokbarak speakers. Subsequently, in 1977 Sri Dasarath Debbarma wrote a book "Why Bengali script is needed for writing Kokbarak". In it he strongly argues for the acceptance of the Bengali Script for writing Kokbarak. Later on he became the education minister and chief minister of Tripura and Kokbarak texts books written in Bengali scripts became quite common in schools in Tripura. Successive Leftist governments thereafter appointed Kokbarak teachers and made provisions for all official supports for its all round promotion.

Roman script

On the other side of the picture, educated speakers of Kokbarak came in touch with roman script in course of their education in convent schools, through text books and study materials of Christian religion. The Baptist Mission at Arundhati Nagar, Agartala, played a substantial role in promoting the use of roman scripts for Kokbarak. Beside religious patronage, supporters of roman scripts also received political patronage from various rightist and extremist tribal outfits like TUJS, TNV, IPFT, NLFT, ATTF etc. These forces have succeeded in introducing textbooks in roman scripts for Kokbarak in the schools within the Tripura Tribal Areas Autonomous District Council (TTADC). A number of English medium residential schools have also come up within the TTADC.

Ambivalence

At present written Kokbarak shows an ambivalent picture in which both roman and Bengali scripts are being used. And there is no doubt that the Kokbarak writers are divided between the two script groups according to their political and religious affiliations: Leftists and non-Christians going for Bengali scripts while the Rightists and Christians preferring to write in roman scripts. Sri Chaudhury concludes his article by anticipating an analogy between Hindusthani and Kokbark: both having two versions depending on the scripts. Hindi is written in devnagari scripts while Urdu is written in Arabic scripts.

Discussion

We have so far discussed in detail two sub-issues in relation to the issue of identity quest of the tribal people of Tripura. There is a third one in this connection which I have just mentioned in passing namely the formation of the TTADC. While the first two are closely linked - related to language - the third one refers to a more crucial aspect of identity formation i.e. a location or place of one's own. On the surface of it, all these are innocuous demands that are often thrown up by the subalterns in a system of liberal democracy. Fulfilling these demands is tantamount to according fundamental recognition to these marginalized sections of the society. But one cannot afford to forgo a word of caution in this respect. This is that, the apparently harmless demands for ethno-linguistic identity can easily be a disguise for some hidden and vested interests supplied clandestinely by alternative center/s of power.

Take for instance the issue of script for Kokbarak again. It is obvious that, those who are backing up the cause of roman script are guided directly or indirectly by their political and religious mentors. Whatever the mass support this cause is enjoying can be interpreted as reflection of a collective psychology of the marginalized. In an effort to assert their independent identity they want to move farthest from the existing center that they view as hegemonic in character. So to oppose Hinduism they prefer Christianity, and to oppose Bengali script they fall for roman script. The equation is quite straight: Hinduism goes with Bengali script when Christianity with roman script! One must remember that this polarization within the tribal folks of Tripura did not surface in course of the movement for recognition of Kokbarak language or formation of TTADC. This asymmetry needs a closer analysis.

Demands for Kokbarak as a language to represent the tribes of Tripura and the demand for formation of TTADC did not suffer much setback from any divisive corner from among the tribal folks presumably because those demands were much more fundamental and spontaneous in character. Man needs language primarily for communication with the members of his community and for this oral communication is basic and has the advantage of spontaneity, a prerequisite for natural linguistic communication: written communication is always secondary and can wait. Similarly, the need for a well-protected homestead is one of the fundamental requirements of self-identity, be it for a nation or an individual. This is why the various tribes of Tripura could put up a united front to fight for Kokbarak and the autonomous district council. By contrast the need for a common script is born out of the necessity for written communication, which is always secondary. The latter lacks the spontaneity and urgency of oral communication, is contingent upon a particular level of literacy, and its need is felt primarily by the educated section of the tribal people.

Picture of education among the tribal people in Tripura opens up yet another facet of the problem under study. The majority of the schools in tribal areas offer primary education through Bengali language and script. Since 1960 or 70s the English medium schools started coming up under the patronage of the Church in the farflung nooks and corners of Tripura. Tribal youths educated in these schools pursue higher and technical education mostly outside Tripura where they do not get the Bengali language or culture. So, these students return to Tripura for job with a language, which is either English or Hindi. They take shelter under these non-Bengali languages to ward off any aggression from the hegemony of the latter. The demand for introduction of roman scripts for writing Kokbarak is mainly aired by this section of the tribal intelligentsia. By contrast, those who availed of the Bengali medium instruction at school (and they are the majority) and are familiar with the Bengali script prefer to use Bengali script. Seen in this light the demand for roman scripts for Kokbarak is rather an elitist one, supported and patronized mainly by the upcoming middle class among the tribal population. It is no surprise then that the leftist tribal leaders always supported the cause of Bengali script because of its mass acceptability.

Coming back to the issue of asserting one's identity through script, it should now be clear why the demand for either Bengali or roman script failed to acquire the proportion of a spontaneous mass movement: script is required only for the written and hence secondary representation of the language. By comparison, the demand for roman script remained a confined one because of its elitist nature while the use of Bengali script enjoys a much wider mass base in addition to official patronage. There is no denying the fact that those who use the Bengali script, far outnumber those who use roman script. And the message should be clear to all concerned. It is the liking or disliking of the majority that decide the fate of linguistic phenomenon for a natural language. Any effort towards any sort of imposition is an exercise in vain if not outright counter productive.

How far de-centering is democratic?

Demand for self-identity and resistance to homogenization is definitely democratic and should be appreciated. But then why does one notice a dubious approach of the Kokbarak speakers towards the linguistic identity of minor tribes of Tripura who do not speak Kokbarak? One cannot fail to notice that the Reangs have already formed a separate organization for asserting their distinct ethno-linguistic identity. So have the Chakmas, the Lushais etc. The Santals and Mundas can in no foreseeable time be expected to accept Kokbarak as their lingua franca! Does it mean that the languages of all of these minor tribes should be given independent official status? Is it at all practicable on the part of any government however democratic might be its character?

Only nine of the nineteen tribes speak Kokbarak and yet the latter is accorded the lingua franca status. Obviously the social, political, economic and demographic predominance of the Kokbarak speakers played a decisive role in pushing their cause through. Standardization of Kokbarak automatically has spelt out once again the marginalized status for the minor tribes. So out of the need to safeguard their ethnolinguistic identity they have started forming alternative centers away from the hegemony of the existing center, in this case Kokbarak.

Those for whom this step is impossible, are either surrendering to the forces of homogenization of Kokbark or leading a life of virtual incognito far away from the mainstream of national and state life, for example, the Santals and Mundas. This is certainly an unsavory picture as far as the democratic value of coexisting heterogeneity is concerned. For the sake of social existence, for the sake of togetherness and for the sake of checking any trigger-happy balkanization of the various spheres of our social existence this sacrifice is a must. This is particularly true of all multiethnic and multilingual societies.

On another occasion, I have argued for adopting a more accommodative and integrative approach towards the minor tribal languages by those who use Kokbarak language, at least for formal purposes. For this I also suggested a sort of 'planned borrowing' from the minor tribal languages so that the latter get a space of their own within the flux of mainstream language culture. This measure has the potential to forestall any further de-centering or creation of new centers of identity at the cost of the existing ones.

I extend the same argument to the script issue. In a heterogeneous society, wherever possible there would be demands for formation of new centers of identity. This process, termed as de-centering in the postmodern discourse, threatens to be a perpetual one since more often than not these minority groups fall prey to sentiments as far as their ethno-linguistic identity is concerned. More dangerously, very often they stand exposed to blackmailing by more powerful alternative centers of interest: for instance, the apparently democratic movement for roman script for Kokbarak actually stems from religious and political groups who remain behind the screen. Additionally, the quest and struggle for identity always produce a serial reaction and sets example for everybody. This creates a mad frenzy for the funny game of perpetual de-centering accompanied by concomitant subversive theorizing and activities.

Such a subversive frenzy should not be equated with democratic demands for identity. The latter is characterized by mass support and their fulfillment promises to satisfy the democratic urge of the majority.

It is time we understood this crucial distinction. Otherwise any centrifugal activity would be wrongly interpreted as democratic, not subversive. In the post-modem world of today all disintegrative forces get encouraged in the name of identity quest for the marginalized. One has to be very alert, therefore, to distinguish between a genuinely democratic demand and one born among the minority out of vested interests, which are detrimental to man's collective existence despite multidimensional heterogeneity. It should now be clear why the movement for recognition of Kokbarak and the formation of TTADC were mass movements, while the script issue has failed to be one.

Conclusion

In a multiethnic and multilingual society, demand for identity especially from the minority and the marginalized is a commonplace phenomenon. While some of these demands are democratic in nature, most of them turn out to be pseudo-democratic and hence, divisive. It is the mass base of a demand that crucially defines if the latter is democratic or divisive in nature. A mere balkanization of the collective life for the sake of experimenting with western post-modem theories, is a game of frenzy and needs to be checked. Alternative centers with hidden motives are always ready to fish in the troubled water. The paper therefore argues against the practice of de-centering for the sake of decentering. Through a comparative analysis of the three major demands of the tribal people in Tripura — for Kokbarak, for TTADC and for a script - I attempt to illustrate the distinction between democratic versus divisive nature of the demands.

Notes

1. This paper was first presented at National seminar on "Development of Tribal Languages: Sharing of Experiences" on 27-28 May, 2006, organized at Agartala, by Govt. of Tripura in collaboration with CILL and the Ministry of Tribal Affairs, Govt. of India. I am grateful to the audience for their valuable comments that certainly enhanced the quality of the paper.

References

Abbi, Anvita. 1997. Introduction. *Languages of Tribal and Indigenous Peoples of India: The Ethnic Space.* Delhi: Motilal Banarsidass.

Chattopadhaya, Suhash. 1972. *Tripurar KokBarak bhashar likhitorupe uttaran.* (as mentioned in Chaudhury, 2006)

Chaudhury, Kumud Kundu. 2006. 'Kokbarak bhashay lipir bikash' in *Tripurar bhasha charcha: Bangla o Kokbarak:* 55-70. Agartala and Kolkata: Akkhor Publications.

Das, Shyamal. 2006. Standardization or the Politics of Marginalization. In *Proceedings of the ICHR National Seminar on "The Tribes, Peasants and Modern Identity in the North Eastern India* (to appear). New Delhi: ICHR and also in this volume.

Debbarma, Dasarath. 1995. *Why Bengali script is needed for writing Kokbarak?* Agartala.

Naisr, V. Saratchandran. 2001. Linguistic Rights of Minorities and Social Justice. In *PILC Journal of Dravidic Studies* 11 *(112):* 93-98. Pondicherry: Pondicherry Institute of Linguistics and Culture.

Rajawat, Mamta. 2001. *Burning Issues of Human Rights.* New Delhi: Kalpaz Publications.

Index

■■■